Ron Wight

KEY PORTER BOOKS

Copyright © 2001 by Ron Wight

All rights reserved. No part of this work covered by the copyrights hereon may be reproduced or used in any form or by any means—graphic, electronic or mechanical, including photocopying, recording, taping or information storage and retrieval systems—without the prior written permission of the publisher, or in the case of photocopying or other reprographic copying, a license from the Canadian Copyright Licensing Agency.

National Library of Canadian Cataloguing in Publication Data

Wight, Ron
The greatest hockey quiz book ever

ISBN 1-55263-333-0

1. Hockey – Miscellanea. 2. National Hockey League – Miscellanea.
I. Title.

GV847.W49 2001   796.962'64   C2001-900618-7

The publisher gratefully acknowledges the support of the Canada Council for the Arts and the Ontario Arts Council for its publishing program.

Canada

We acknowledge the financial support of the Government of Canada through the Book Publishing Industry Development Program (BPIDP) for our publishing activities.

Acknowlegments: I would like to thank my family—Jodie, who shares my passion for the game, and Carly and Cindy, who love and support me in spite of it. Without your help, this book would never have become a reality.

Key Porter Books Limited
70 The Esplanade
Toronto, Ontario
Canada M5E 1R2

www.keyporter.com

Design and electronic formatting: Lightfoot Art & Design Inc.
Photo credit: All photographs courtesy of Hockey Hall of Fame

Printed and bound in Canada

01 02 03 04 05 06 6 5 4 3 2 1

CONTENTS

Introduction	5
Game 1: The Cup Quest (The Stanley Cup Playoffs)	7
Game 2: Beginnings (Hockey to 1926)	22
Game 3: One League (1926 to 1955)	41
Game 4: A Tale of Two Cities (1955 to 1967)	58
Game 5: Arrival (and a Rival) of Expansion (1967 to 1979)	74
Game 6: The Wayne and Mario Show (1979 to 1993)	92
Game 7: Heading South (1993 to 2001)	109
Game 8: The Honor Roll (Records and Awards)	125
Game 9: A Global Game (International Hockey)	143

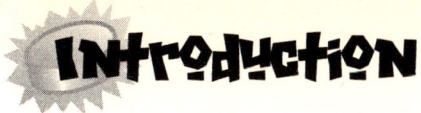

INTRODUCTION

Since the time I was a very young boy, I have found hockey fascinating. The game has become a part of me. Whether playing or watching it, I am intrigued by its details and intricacies.

When I was seven, I received my first hockey book. Since then, hockey history has become my hobby. The game of hockey has evolved over time, growing and developing as leagues have formed and dissolved. The players have come and gone; some stars, some journeymen, some builders.

I hope this book, as it challenges your ability in the trivia of hockey, also provides in its questions and answers an overview of the course the game has taken. It truly has been an amazing journey.

Ron Wight

Game 1: The Cup Quest

The Stanley Cup Playoffs

More than 100 years ago, when he paid 10 guineas (about $50) for it, Lord Stanley had no idea how important his silver trophy would become. So let's start with some of the stories of those who have fought for this icon of hockey supremacy for more than a century.

First Period: Who Am I?

1. I am the only non-Canadian to win the Conn Smythe Trophy as the most valuable player to his team in the Stanley Cup playoffs.

Brian Leetch, an American, was named the most valuable player in the 1994 playoffs as his offensive skills led the New York Rangers to their first Stanley Cup victory since 1940.

2. I played on six Stanley Cup winners during the eight NHL seasons from 1961–62 to 1968–69.

Dick Duff played for the Toronto Maple Leafs when they won in 1962 and 1963, and then the Montreal Canadiens in 1965, 1966, 1968 and 1969.

3. I hold the record for scoring a goal in the highest number of consecutive games in a single playoff season.

Reg Leach of the Philadelphia Flyers scored in 10 consecutive games during the 1976 playoffs, recording 15 goals against Toronto, Boston and Montreal during his scoring streak.

4. I am the first winner of the Conn Smythe Trophy as the most valuable player in the playoffs.
Jean Beliveau was with the Montreal Canadiens in 1965. He recorded 16 points in 13 playoff games as he captained the Habs to the Cup.

5. I won nine Stanley Cups as a player, but I haven't been voted into the Hockey Hall of Fame.
Claude Provost was a member of nine Cup winners in the 1950s and 1960s and a First Team All–Star for 1964–65, but this superb checking forward still hasn't made it to the Hockey Hall of Fame.

6. I am the only coach to lead two different NHL franchises to consecutive Stanley Cup victories.
Tommy Gorman coached the 1934 Chicago Black Hawks and the 1935 Montreal Maroons.

7. I am the only person to win three consecutive Stanley Cups as the coach and GM.
George "Punch" Imlach was the coach and general manager of the Toronto Maple Leafs when they won the Stanley Cup in 1962, 1963 and 1964.

8. While I played in only one game in the 1951–52 regular season—my last in the NHL—I took part in two playoff games at the end of it.
Walter "Turk" Broda spent 30 minutes in goal in the last game of the 1951–52 season but then played two complete games in the semifinals.

9. I am the only goaltender to play in three seventh and deciding games in the Stanley Cup finals.
Terry Sawchuk was in goal for the Detroit Red Wings in the seventh game of the Stanley Cup finals in 1954, 1955 and 1964.

10. I am the first individual to coach both an American- and a Canadian-based team to a Stanley Cup victory.
Lester Patrick coached the Cup-winning Victoria Cougars (in 1925) and New York Rangers (in 1928).

11. We played in the highest number of NHL seasons without winning the Stanley Cup.

Both Dean Prentice and Doug Mohns participated in 22 NHL seasons without being on a Cup winner.

12. I played on a Stanley Cup winner in my first full NHL season with Toronto and my last one with Chicago.

Tod Sloan was a member of the 1950–51 Toronto Maple Leafs and the 1960–61 Chicago Black Hawks.

13. I hold the record for playing in the most Stanley Cup playoff seasons.

The participation of Colorado's Ray Bourque in the 2001 Stanley Cup playoffs marked his record 21st year in post-season competition. His lone absence occurred in 1997, when Bourque's Boston Bruins missed the playoffs.

14. I coached the Detroit Red Wings to a Stanley Cup in my first year of coaching in the NHL.

Jimmy Skinner coached the Red Wings to a Stanley Cup in 1954–55.

15. I recorded the highest number of career overtime goals in the Stanley Cup playoffs.

Maurice "Rocket" Richard had a career total of six playoff overtime goals: one in 1946, three in 1951, one in 1957 and one in 1958.

16. I hold the record for playing the most playoff games with the Chicago Black Hawks.

Stan Mikita participated in 155 playoff games over 18 post-seasons as a Black Hawk.

17. I scored the fastest overtime goal in Stanley Cup playoff history.

Brian Skrudland scored at nine seconds of overtime in the second game of the Stanley Cup finals on May 18, 1986, to give Montreal a 3–2 win. Montreal went on to defeat Calgary in the best-of-seven series four games to one.

18. I led the NHL's playoff scoring race in both of the years that my Philadelphia Flyers won the Stanley Cup, 1974 and 1975.

Rick MacLeish led scorers with 13 goals and 9 assists for 22 points in 17 games in the 1974 Stanley Cup playoffs (including the only goal in the Flyers' 1–0 Cup-clinching win in game six) and 11 goals and 9 assists for 20 points in 17 games in 1975.

19. I am the only player to spend my entire playing career with one team—and to win a Stanley Cup in both my first NHL season and again, more than 10 years later, in my last one.
  Jacques Lemaire was a member of the Cup-winning Montreal Canadiens in 1967–68 and was still with them in 1978–79.

20. I am the only player to have my name inscribed on the Stanley Cup a record 11 times.
  Henri Richard played for the Montreal Canadiens in 11 Cup-winning seasons.

Second Period: Multiple Choice

1. Name the first U.S.-based team to win the Stanley Cup.
a) The Portland Rosebuds b) The Seattle Metropolitans
c) The Boston Bruins d) The New York Rangers
  b) The Seattle Metropolitans defeated the Montreal Canadiens in the Stanley Cup finals in 1917.

2. Which team was the first NHL Cup winner?
a) The Toronto Arenas b) The Montreal Canadiens
c) The Ottawa Senators d) The Quebec Bulldogs
  a) The Toronto Arenas won the first NHL Stanley Cup in 1918 when they defeated the Vancouver Millionaires of the Pacific Coast Hockey Association (PCHA).

3. How many times have the Stanley Cup finals gone to a game seven?
a) 8   b) 9   c) 10   d) 11
  d) 11.

Game Sevens of Stanley Cup Finals
April 18, 1942	Detroit 1 at Toronto 3
April 22, 1945	Detroit 1 at Toronto 2
April 23, 1950	New York Rangers 3 at Detroit 4 (overtime)

April 16, 1954	Montreal 1 at Detroit 2 (overtime)
April 14, 1955	Montreal 1 at Detroit 3
April 25, 1964	Detroit 0 at Toronto 4
May 1, 1965	Chicago 0 at Montreal 4
May 18, 1971	Montreal 3 at Chicago 2
May 31, 1987	Philadelphia 1 at Edmonton 3
June 14, 1994	Vancouver 2 at New York Rangers 3
June 9, 2001	New Jersey 1 at Colorado 3

4. On how many occasions have all of the Original Six teams qualified for the Stanley Cup playoffs?
a) 4   b) 5   c) 6   d) 7

c) 6. All of the Original Six franchises qualified for the Stanley Cup playoffs in 1941, 1942, 1978, 1987, 1994 and 1996.

5. How many times have teams from the same city won both the Stanley Cup and the Memorial Cup as Canada's junior hockey champion in the same year?
a) 2   b) 3   c) 4   d) 5

d) 5. Teams from Toronto won both trophies in 1945 and 1947 (the Maple Leafs and St. Michael's Majors) and again in 1964 and 1967 (the Maple Leafs and the Marlboros). In 1969, the Montreal Canadiens won the Stanley Cup and the Junior Canadiens won the Memorial Cup.

6. Which NHL team holds the record for consecutive playoff appearances?
a) Boston   b) Chicago   c) Montreal   d) Toronto

a) Boston made a record 29 consecutive playoff appearances between 1968 and 1996.

7. How many playoff games in NHL history have gone into five or more overtime periods?
a) 2   b) 3   c) 4   d) 5

b) 3.

Overtime	Date	Result	Overtime Scorer
116:30	March 24, 1936	Detroit 1 at Montreal Maroons 0	Mud Bruneteau
104:46	April 3, 1933	Boston 0 at Toronto 1	Ken Doraty
92:01	May 4, 2000	Philadelphia 2 at Pittsburgh 1	Keith Primeau

8. How many times has the Stanley Cup-winning goal been scored by that year's Conn Smythe Trophy winner?
a) 6   b) 7   c) 8   d) 9

   a) 6. Jean Beliveau in 1965, Bobby Orr in 1970 and 1972, Yvan Cournoyer in 1973, Mike Bossy in 1982 and Wayne Gretzky in 1988 are the only five players to score the Stanley Cup-winning goal and win the Conn Smythe Trophy in the same playoff year.

9. How many times has the Hart Trophy (for the NHL's most valuable player in the regular season) and the Conn Smythe Trophy (for the MVP in the Stanley Cup playoffs) been awarded to the same individual in the same season?
a) 4   b) 5   c) 6   d) 7

   a) 4. Bobby Orr was awarded both trophies in 1970 and 1972, Guy Lafleur achieved the feat in 1977, and Wayne Gretzky won both the Hart and Conn Smythe awards in 1985.

10. On how many occasions has an NHL team with a losing regular-season record won the Stanley Cup?
a) 0   b) 1   c) 2   d) 3

   c) 2. The 1937–38 Chicago Black Hawks, with 14–25–9, and the 1948–49 Toronto Maple Leafs, with 22–25–13, are the only two teams with regular-season records below .500 to win the Stanley Cup.

11. What is the highest number of Stanley Cup championships for an individual NHL goalie?
a) 5   b) 6   c) 7   d) 8

   b) 6. Two goalies have participated in six Stanley Cup victories—and both were Montreal Canadiens. Jacques Plante participated in the 1953, 1956, 1957, 1958, 1959 and 1960 Cup-winning teams and Ken Dryden was with the 1971, 1973, 1976, 1977, 1978 and 1979 Canadiens.

12. How many times was Wayne Gretzky the leading scorer in the Stanley Cup playoffs?
a) 5   b) 6   c) 7   d) 8

   b) 6. Gretzky was the leading playoff scorer as an Edmonton Oiler in 1983, 1984, 1985, 1987 and 1988 and again in 1993 with the Los Angeles Kings.

13. Which of the following players skated for Boston during all three of the Bruins' first Stanley Cup victories?
a) Dit Clapper   b) Eddie Shore
c) Tiny Thompson   d) Ralph "Cooney" Weiland

a) Dit Clapper participated in Boston's Stanley Cup victories in 1929, 1939 and 1941. Eddie Shore played in both 1929 and 1939 but was traded to the New York Americans in January 1940 and missed the Bruins' 1941 Cup. Tiny Thompson was the goaltender for the 1929 Cup but was traded to Detroit early in the 1938–39 season, making way for Frank Brimsek. Cooney Weiland played for the Bruins in 1929 and 1939, but he retired after the 1939 Cup. He took over the Bruins' coaching and won the Cup in that capacity in 1941.

14. Approximately 53%—or 16 of 30—of the NHL's teams qualified for the playoffs in the 2000–2001 season. What was the highest percentage of NHL teams to qualify for the playoffs in a season?
a) 71%   b) 75%   c) 76%   d) 86%

d) 86%. Six of the NHL's seven teams qualified for the playoffs in the four seasons from 1938–39 to 1941–42; six of eight teams (75%) qualified from 1935–36 to 1937–38; 12 of 17 teams (71%) qualified during 1978–79; and 16 of 21 teams (76%) qualified from 1979–80 to 1990–91.

15. There has been only one playoff year since the 1926–27 season, when the NHL took sole ownership of the Stanley Cup, that there hasn't been a single overtime game in the playoffs. Which year was it?
a) 1933   b) 1943   c) 1953   d) 1963

d) 1963. None of the 16 playoff games went into overtime that year for the first and only time from 1926–27 to the present.

16. What is the highest number of consecutive seasons that the Stanley Cup winner has swept the best-of-seven final series?
a) 3   b) 4   c) 5   d) 6

b) 4. The Stanley Cup was swept in four straight on four successive occasions between 1995 and 1998: New Jersey defeated Detroit in 1995; Colorado beat Florida in 1996; Detroit swept Philadelphia in 1997; and Detroit won over Washington in 1998.

17. When the Detroit Red Wings finally captured the Stanley Cup in 1997, it marked the end of a 42-year drought dating back to their last Cup in 1955. How many times had Detroit lost the finals in the years in between?
a) 2   b) 4   c) 6   d) 8

   c) 6. The Red Wings lost the Cup in five games to Montreal in 1956, in six games to Chicago in 1961, in five games to Toronto in 1963, in seven games to Toronto in 1964, in six games to Montreal in 1966 and in four games to New Jersey in 1995.

18. On how many occasions has an NHL franchise won the Stanley Cup in one season but failed to qualify for the playoffs in the following year?
a) 2   b) 4   c) 6   d) 8

   d) 8. Toronto holds the distinction of having this happen on four separate occasions. The following Stanley Cup winners failed to qualify for the playoffs in the following season:

Stanley Cup Winner	Stanley Cup Season	Missed Playoffs
The Toronto Arenas	1917–18	1918–19
The Toronto St. Pats	1921–22	1922–23
The Detroit Red Wings	1936–37	1937–38
The Chicago Black Hawks	1937–38	1938–39
The Toronto Maple Leafs	1944–45	1945–46
The Toronto Maple Leafs	1966–67	1967–68
The Montreal Canadiens	1968–69	1969–70
The New Jersey Devils	1994–95	1995–96

19. How many times have teams from Montreal and Calgary met in the Stanley Cup finals?
a) 2   b) 3   c) 4   d) 5

   b) 3. The Montreal Canadiens defeated the Calgary Tigers of the Western Canada Hockey League (WCHL) in two straight games by scores of 6–1 and 3–0 in the 1924 finals. The next time the two cities met in the finals was in 1986, when the Canadiens defeated the Calgary Flames four games to one to capture the Cup. The last meeting to date was in 1989, when the Calgary Flames defeated Montreal four games to two for the only Cup that Calgary has won.

Bill Barilko's 1951 Cup-winning overtime goal, followed by his disappearance in Northern Ontario, enshrined his place in hockey history.

20. How many Stanley Cup final series did Gordie Howe play in?
a) 8   b) 9   c) 10   d) 11

c) 10. Gordie Howe played in the Stanley Cup finals in 1948, 1949, 1952, 1954, 1955, 1956, 1961, 1963, 1964 and 1966. The Red Wings also made the finals in 1950, but Howe suffered a nearly fatal head injury in the semifinals that kept him out of the finals against the New York Rangers.

Third Period: Expert Trivia

1. When the New Jersey Devils captured the 2000 Stanley Cup, it marked a record seventh consecutive win by an American-based team. When had teams located in the U.S. achieved a string of six Cup victories prior to 1994–99?

From 1936 to 1941, the Cup was won by Detroit (1936, 1937), Chicago (1938), Boston (1939 and 1941) and the New York Rangers (1940). The Montreal Maroons had won in 1935 and Toronto ended the American streak in 1942.

2. Name the last non-NHL team to win the Cup.

The 1925 Victoria Cougars of the Western Canada Hockey League defeated the Montreal Canadiens—and were also the last non-NHL Cup finalists. They returned to the finals in 1926, when they lost to the Montreal Maroons.

3. Name the only two NHL defensemen to win the playoff scoring race. (Hint: They both won the Conn Smythe Trophy in the same year they led playoff scoring.)

Al MacInnis of the Calgary Flames recorded 31 points in 22 games in the 1989 playoffs and Brian Leetch recorded 34 points in 23 games for the New York Rangers in the 1994 post-season. On three other occasions, defensemen tied for the scoring race but actually placed second because another player had a higher goal total. Bobby Orr's 24 points tied Phil Esposito's in the 1972 playoffs and Cy Wentworth's 5 points matched Baldy Northcott's and Harvey Jackson's in 1935. Pierre Pilote's 15 tied Gordie Howe's in 1961.

4. When was the best-of-seven format first used in the Stanley Cup playoffs?

The first best-of-seven series in Stanley Cup playoff history went the full seven games as the Boston Bruins defeated the New York Rangers four games to three in the semifinal matchup in the 1939 playoffs.

5. Name the two Boston players whose names are on the Cup who didn't play for the Bruins during the Cup-winning seasons.

Hal Winkler is listed as one of the 1928–29 champions. He had retired the year before, and the Bruins included him on the Cup as a backup/practice goalie. Ted Green is listed as a member of the 1969–70 Bruins, but he had been injured in a pre-season game on September 21, 1969, and was out for the whole season.

6. Name the smallest city or town to win the Stanley Cup.

The Thistles from Kenora won the Stanley Cup in 1907.

7. In which seasons have all NHL playoff series been best-of-seven series?

Every year from 1943 to 1974 and from 1987 to 2001 has had all playoff series in the best-of-seven format.

8. What was the longest game seven in Stanley Cup playoff history?

The New York Islanders defeated the Washington Capitals on April 18, 1987, with a score of 3–2 when Pat LaFontaine scored at 8:47 of the fourth overtime period—a few seconds before 2 a.m.

9. When did a father last coach a son in the Stanley Cup finals?

Lester Patrick coached the New York Rangers when his son Lynn played in the finals and Detroit defeated New York in five games in 1937. Lynn played for the Rangers in the finals again in 1940, but Frank Boucher had taken over the coaching and Patrick was the general manager.

10. Bill Goldsworthy of the Minnesota North Stars led playoff scoring with 15 points in 1968, while Phil Esposito of the Boston Bruins was the leading scorer with 18 points in the 1969 playoffs. But, neither the 1967–68 Minnesota North Stars nor the 1968–69 Boston Bruins advanced to the Stanley

Cup finals. On only two occasions since then has the playoff scoring race been won by players who didn't participate in the finals. Name the years and the players involved.

In 1986, the St. Louis Blues didn't advance to the finals, but the leading playoff scorers were Doug Gilmour and Bernie Federko, who both recorded 21 points in the 19 games the Blues played. The Blues lost in a seven-game semifinal to the Calgary Flames and the Montreal Canadiens defeated the Flames in the finals. In 1999, Peter Forsberg of the Colorado Avalanche led the playoff scoring with 24 points in 19 games, but the Avalanche went down in seven games to the Dallas Stars in the conference finals and Dallas went on to defeat the Buffalo Sabres.

11. Which of the Original Six arenas saw the most Stanley Cup victories?

Arena	NHL Service	Stanley Cup Victories	Years
Montreal Forum	1924–96	16	1926, 1928, 1930, 1931, 1935, 1944, 1946, 1953, 1956, 1957, 1959, 1965, 1968, 1979, 1989, 1993
Maple Leaf Gardens	1931–99	12	1932, 1933, 1936, 1940, 1942, 1947, 1949, 1951, 1960, 1963, 1964, 1967
Detroit Olympia	1927–79	10	1937, 1941, 1945, 1948, 1950, 1952, 1954, 1955, 1961, 1966
Boston Garden	1928–95	7	1939, 1943, 1958, 1970, 1977, 1978, 1990
Chicago Stadium	1929–94	6	1934, 1938, 1962, 1971, 1973, 1992
Madison Square Garden	1925–68	1	1929

12. The Original Six era began in 1942–43 and the NHL abandoned the best-of-three playoff series that season. When did the NHL reintroduce the best-of-three format on a limited basis?

For the five seasons from 1974–75 to 1978–79, the NHL held four best-of-three preliminary round playoffs to eliminate four of the 12 teams that qualified for the playoffs and leave eight for the quarterfinals.

13. Has a former Chicago player ever coached the Hawks to a Stanley Cup championship?

No. In fact, only two former players have ever taken the Black Hawks to the final series. Dick Irvin played with Chicago from 1926 to 1929 and coached the Hawks to the final series in 1931, when Montreal defeated them three games to two in the finals. Paul Thompson played with Chicago from 1931 to 1939 and coached the Hawks in 1944, when they lost four straight to Montreal in the finals.

14. Name the only NHL season in which no Canadian team qualified for the Stanley Cup playoffs.

In 1969–70, the only two Canadian teams (Montreal and Toronto) finished fifth and sixth in the Eastern Division and failed to qualify for the Stanley Cup playoffs.

15. What was the latest date in the year for a Stanley Cup win?

June 24, 1995. New Jersey defeated Detroit 5–2 to win the Cup in four games in 1995 when a lockout delayed the regular season. The playoffs didn't begin until May 6 of that year.

16. Name the most northern and the most southern site of a Stanley Cup victory.

The northernmost site of a Stanley Cup victory is Edmonton and the Cup was won there in 1984, 1985, 1987 and 1988. The southernmost site is Miami, Florida, where Colorado defeated the Panthers in 1996.

17. What is the largest margin of victory in an NHL deciding game for the Cup?

Pittsburgh defeated Minnesota 8–0 in the deciding game (game six) in 1991.

18. Name the last time that all of the games of a Stanley Cup final took place in one rink.

The New York Rangers and the Montreal Maroons played all five games in the Montreal Forum in 1928 when the Rangers had to move out of their home rink because the circus was making its annual visit to Madison Square Garden.

19. Since the Stanley Cup became the sole property of the NHL in 1927, only three playoff games in the finals have ended without a winner being determined. When did they take place? (Hint: The Boston Bruins took part in all three.)
April 7, 1927: Ottawa 0 at Boston 0
  (game called in second overtime, poor ice)
April 11, 1927: Boston 1 at Ottawa 1
  (game called after first overtime, poor ice)
May 24, 1988: Edmonton 3 at Boston 3
  (game called in second period, power failure)

20. What was the first American-based NHL team to take part in a playoff game?
On March 20, 1926, the Montreal Maroons at Pittsburgh Pirates, Maroons 3, Pirates 1.

Overtime: Four on Four

1. The Montreal Canadiens have won the Stanley Cup on an overtime goal on four occasions. Name the four players who scored the overtime goals.
Toe Blake, Elmer Lach, Henri Richard and Jacques Lemaire. Toe Blake scored the Stanley Cup-winning goal on April 13, 1944, at 9:12 of the first overtime period to give Montreal a 5–4 win over Chicago and sweep the series in four straight games. Elmer Lach scored at 1:22 on April 16, 1953, to give Montreal a 1–0 win over the Boston Bruins and a series win of four games to one. Henri Richard scored a controversial goal against Detroit's Roger Crozier at 2:20 of overtime on May 5, 1966, to give Montreal a 3–2 game and a 4–2 series win. Jacques Lemaire scored at 4:32 of overtime on May 14, 1977, to give Montreal a 2–1 win over the Boston Bruins and a four-game sweep in the 1977 Stanley Cup finals.

2. Name the only four NHL players to captain three consecutive Stanley Cup-winning teams.

Maurice "Rocket" Richard, George Armstrong, Yvan Cournoyer and Denis Potvin. Furthermore, three of these four captained four consecutive Cup winners in their first four seasons as captain and two achieved the feat in their last four in the NHL (Richard with the Montreal Canadiens from 1957 through 1960 and Cournoyer from 1976 through 1979). Potvin took over as captain in 1979–80 and the Islanders won four consecutive Cups from 1980 to 1983. George Armstrong was appointed Toronto's captain in 1957–58 and took the Maple Leafs to three consecutive Cup victories from 1962 to 1964.

3. Name the only four individuals to win the Conn Smythe Trophy as the outstanding player in the Stanley Cup playoffs as a member of the losing side.

Roger Crozier (Detroit) in 1966; Glenn Hall (St. Louis) in 1968; Reggie Leach (Philadelphia) in 1976; and Ron Hextall (Philadelphia) in 1987.

4. NHL stars Jack Darragh, Howie Morenz and Toe Blake all scored two Stanley Cup-winning goals in their careers. Name the four NHL players to achieve this feat since.

Jean Beliveau in 1960 and 1965; Henri Richard in 1966 and 1971; Bobby Orr in 1970 and 1972; Mike Bossy in 1982 and 1983.

Game 2: Beginnings

Hockey to 1926

The origins of this wonderful game continue to stir impassioned debate. What we do know is that leagues were well established in Montreal in the 1880s and the Stanley Cup was first awarded in 1893. Hockey evolved from an amateur to a professional game in the early years of the 20th century, with the National Hockey Association establishing itself as the elite league for the 1909–1910 season. The rival Pacific Coast Hockey Association began play in 1911–12 and the two leagues competed for the top professionals available. The NHA was transformed into the National Hockey League for the 1917–18 season, while the PCHA was amalgamated into the Western Canada Hockey League in the 1924–25 season and became known as the Western Hockey League in 1925–26. The WHL folded after that year, leaving the NHL as the sole elite professional hockey league in North America and the only competitors for the Stanley Cup.

First Period: Who Am I?

1. I played 328 consecutive regular-season games in goal before I had to leave a game in November 1925.

Georges Vezina played 328 consecutive games with Montreal from 1910–11 until the first game of the 1925–26 season. He left after the first period of a game against Pittsburgh on November 28, 1925, and died of tuberculosis the following March.

2. I am the first player to record more than 100 penalty minutes in an NHL season.

Bert Corbeau recorded 121 penalty minutes in 36 games with the Toronto St. Pats in 1925–26. And this was the second time he'd garnered the dubious distinction of spending the most time in the box. In 1923–24, he'd incurred 55 penalty minutes.

3. I was the goaltender for the Montreal Wanderers in their only four NHL games and played 16 games with the Toronto Arenas the following season. (Hint: My son went on to become a Hall of Fame left winger.)

Bert Lindsay played in 20 NHL games in 1917–18 and 1918–19, but he also had a lengthy professional goaltending career with such teams as the Renfrew Creamery Kings of the Federal Hockey League and NHA, the Renfrew Millionaires of the NHA and the Victoria Aristocrats of the PCHA before he finally moved on to the Montreal Wanderers of the NHA and then the NHL. His son Ted became a star in the Original Six era.

4. I was the goaltender for the famed Dawson City Klondikers of 1905.

Seventeen-year-old Albert Forrest was in the Klondikers' net for their two losses (9–2, 23–2) to the Ottawa Silver Seven in January 1905.

5. I was the first coach of an NHL Stanley Cup champion.

Dick Carroll was the rookie coach of the 1917–18 Toronto Arenas who defeated the Vancouver Millionaires of the PCHA in five games in the 1918 Stanley Cup finals.

6. I was the captain of the famed Ottawa Silver Seven who held the Stanley Cup from March 1903 to March 1906.

Harvey Pulford was an outstanding athlete in other sports—football, rowing, lacrosse, among others—as well as an outstanding defenseman with Ottawa between 1893–94 and 1907–08. Widely hailed as a capable leader, he captained the team known as the "Silver Seven" during their successful defenses of the Stanley Cup between 1903 and 1905. He is a member of the Hockey Hall of Fame.

7. I led both the NHA and the NHL in goal-scoring twice and was a member of three Stanley Cup-winning teams.

Hall of Famer Joe Malone led the NHA in goals with 43 in 1912–13 and 41 in 1916–17 as a member of the Quebec Bulldogs. He also led the NHL with 44 goals in 1917–18 as a Montreal Canadien and in 1919–20 with 39 goals as a Bulldog (again). He was on the Stanley Cup-winning teams in 1912 and 1913 with the Bulldogs and in his final season, 1923–24, with the Canadiens.

8. I was the only head coach of the Montreal Wanderers in the NHL.

Art Ross went on to become a legend as coach and general manager of the Boston Bruins, but he was coach of the Montreal Wanderers during the NHL's first season, 1917–18. Unfortunately, they only played four games before their arena burned down, at which time the team had a record of one win and three losses.

9. I played in four consecutive Stanley Cup finals between 1917 and 1920.

Harry "Hap" Holmes was a member of the Stanley Cup-winning Seattle Metropolitans in 1917 when they defeated the Montreal Canadiens for the Cup and the Toronto Arenas when they defeated the Vancouver Millionaires in 1918. He was back in goal with Seattle for the 1919 Stanley Cup finals against the Montreal Canadiens in a series that was suspended due to an epidemic of influenza. And he played goal again when Seattle was defeated by Ottawa in the 1920 Stanley Cup finals.

10. I scored five goals in my first NHL game.

Joe Malone scored five goals in the Montreal Canadiens' opening game against the Ottawa Senators on December 19, 1917—his first NHL game because the league was just founded that year—and went on to lead the new league with 44 goals in 20 games in the 1917–18 season.

11. I scored the most goals in a single Stanley Cup playoff game.

One-eyed Frank McGee scored 14 goals in Ottawa's 23–2 victory over Dawson City on January 16, 1905.

12. My third goal of the game in the closing moments allowed the Montreal Victorias to reclaim the Stanley Cup from the Winnipeg Victorias on December 30, 1896. My hat trick was the first recorded in Stanley Cup history.

This was Ernie McLea's first Stanley Cup championship, but he and the Victorias would win again in 1897 and 1898.

13. I was a member of a Stanley Cup team in both my first and my last NHL seasons. I also played in the PCHA for three seasons between my Cup wins.

Jack Adams was a member of the Stanley Cup-winning Toronto Arenas in 1917–18 and the Ottawa Senators in 1926–27. Adams played six of seven NHL seasons with the Toronto Arenas/St. Pats and his final Cup-winning season was with Ottawa. He also played from 1919 to 1922 with the Vancouver Millionaires (and led the PCHA in scoring with 26 goals in 24 games in 1921–22). While Adams was inducted into the Hockey Hall of Fame as a player, he went on to a lengthy career as coach and general manager of the Detroit franchise that ultimately became the Red Wings.

14. I scored the first overtime Cup-winning goal—and I was wearing a mask at the time.

Dan Bain was a great athlete who excelled in many sports and was a member of the Winnipeg Victorias' Stanley Cup championship teams in 1896, 1901 and 1902. In 1901, he captained the Victorias to a two-game victory over the Montreal Shamrocks. Sporting a wooden mask to protect a broken nose, Bain scored a goal in Winnipeg's 4–3 victory over the Shamrocks on January 29, 1901, and both goals, including the winner four minutes into overtime, in a 2–1 victory over the Shamrocks on January 31, 1901.

15. I played for both of the expansion teams (the Boston Bruins and the Montreal Maroons) during the 1924–25 season. The following season, I played with the expansion Pittsburgh Pirates.

Alf Skinner was a veteran of Toronto teams in the NHA and NHL, and a member of the 1918 Stanley Cup-winning Toronto Arenas. He then moved to the PCHA, where he played for Vancouver for five seasons, from 1919–20 to 1923–24. Vancouver traded him to the Boston Bruins prior to the 1924–25 season and the Bruins traded him to their expansion cousins, the Montreal Maroons, in January 1925. He then signed as a free agent with the Pittsburgh Pirates for the 1925–26 season and played his last seven games in the league for them.

Frank McGee scored an incredible fourteen goals in a single Stanley Cup contest in 1905.

16. I am the only person who played on each of the first three Toronto-based Stanley Cup-winning teams.

Hockey Hall of Famer Harry Cameron was a member of the Stanley Cup-winning 1913–14 Toronto Blueshirts of the NHA, the 1917–18 Toronto Arenas of the NHL and the 1921–22 Toronto St. Pats. He played with the St. Pats until the end of the 1922–23 season, then moved on to the Western Canada Hockey League to play with the Saskatoon Crescents. He was inducted into the Hockey Hall of Fame in 1962.

17. I was a member of four Stanley Cup-winning teams and was elected to the Hockey Hall of Fame as a player in 1962. I was also the last person to coach a Hamilton franchise in the NHL.

Jimmy Gardner was a member of four Stanley Cup-winning teams, the Montreal AAA in 1902 and 1903 and the Montreal Wanderers in 1908 and 1910. He both played with and coached the Canadiens in 1913–14 and 1914–15, and finished his playing career as a Canadien during the 1914–15 season. Gardner then refereed for several seasons, including one in the WCHL. He returned to coaching duties with the Hamilton Tigers for the 1924–25 season, which was marred by a season-ending player protest over salaries that resulted in a relocation of the team to New York as the Americans the following season.

18. I was a member of the Montreal Wanderers team that held the Stanley Cup for most of the time between 1906 and 1910. In 1911–12, I moved to the PCHA, where I played for 11 seasons. While I was never on a Cup winner again, I did reach the 1916 Stanley Cup finals as a member of the Portland Rosebuds.

Hall of Famer Moose Johnson was a highly regarded defenseman throughout his career. He was tall and he used a long stick in the days before regulations restricted stick length—adding up to a reach that soon made him notorious.

19. I was the only person to play on both of the Canadiens' first two Stanley Cup-winning teams in 1916 and 1924.

Georges Vezina tended goal in Montreal's Stanley Cup victories in both 1916 and 1924.

20. I was the coach of the Montreal Canadiens for their first Stanley Cup championship.

Newsy Lalonde was player-coach of the 1916 Stanley Cup-winning Canadiens.

Second Period: Multiple Choice

1. What was the first American NHL franchise?
a) The Boston Bruins
b) The Detroit Cougars
c) The Pittsburgh Pirates
d) The New York Americans

a) The Boston Bruins joined the NHL in 1924–25, the Pittsburgh Pirates and New York Americans followed, and the Detroit Cougars (Red Wings), Chicago Black Hawks and New York Rangers joined in 1926–27.

2. Which NHL team was the first to record 20 victories in a single NHL season?
a) The Hamilton Tigers
b) The Montreal Maroons
c) The Ottawa Senators
d) The Toronto St. Pats

c) The Ottawa Senators. Two teams achieved 20 victories in the 1925–26 season when the NHL schedule was increased from 30 to 36 games, but Ottawa achieved the milestone first. They won their 20th game of the season on February 18, 1926, in a 4–2 victory over the Montreal Canadiens at Ottawa. Ottawa went on to win four more games that season and finished with a total of 24 victories. The Montreal Maroons also won 20 games, but their 20th—and final—victory of the season came on March 13, 1926, again with a 4–2 win over the Montreal Canadiens. The Hamilton Tigers and the Toronto St. Pats had both won 19 games in the previous season, 1924–25, as had Ottawa in 1919–20.

3. The Montreal Amateur Athletic Association was the first team to be awarded the Stanley Cup for their winning season in 1892–93. How many times in total did the MAAA win the Stanley Cup?
a) 1
b) 2
c) 3
d) 4

d) 4. They won the Cup in 1893 for first place in the Canadian Amateur Hockey Association with a 7–1–0 record. In 1893–94, they defeated the Montreal Victorias by a score of 3–2 and the Ottawa Capitals by a score of 3–1 to recapture the Cup. In March 1902, they successfully challenged the Winnipeg Victorias in Winnipeg, losing the first game of the series 1–0 but then winning the next two 5–0 and 2–1. In February 1903, they again defeated the Victorias in a challenge held in Montreal. They won the first game 8–1, tied a curfewed second game 2–2, lost the third 4–2 and then won the fourth 4–1.

4. What city was the first to take the Cup away from Montreal?
a) Ottawa   b) Quebec City   c) Toronto   d) Winnipeg

d) The Winnipeg Victorias defeated the Montreal Victorias by a score of 2–0 to win the Stanley Cup on February 14, 1896, in a game played in Montreal. The Cup's stay in Winnipeg was relatively short-lived, however. The Montreal Victorias travelled there to retake it 10 months later by a score of 6–5.

5. What team finally defeated the Ottawa Silver Seven in March 1906 after nine successful defenses of the Cup?
a) The Rat Portage
b) The Montreal Victorias
c) The Montreal Wanderers
d) The Winnipeg Wanderers

c) The Montreal Wanderers defeated Ottawa in a two-game total-goals series held on March 14 and 17, 1906. The Wanderers won the first game by a score of 9–1, but the Silver Seven came back and were winning the second 9–1 when Lester Patrick put two goals in late in the game for a score of 9–3. With an overall advantage of 12 goals to 10, the Wanderers captured the Cup.

6. What is the record for the most goals by one team in a single Stanley Cup playoff game?
a) 23   b) 25   c) 27   d) 29

a) 23. On January 16, 1905, the Ottawa Silver Seven defeated Dawson City 23–2 in the second and final game of a Stanley Cup challenge.

7. How many times has the city of Quebec played in a Stanley Cup championship series?
a) 1   b) 2   c) 3   d) 4

b) 2. Quebec City has been involved in the Stanley Cup finals only twice—and was a winner both times. The 1911–12 and 1912–13 Quebec Bulldogs became Cup champions when they won the NHA title and defeated the winners of the Maritime Professional Hockey League. The city narrowly missed its third championship in 1995–96 when the Nordiques relocated to Denver as the Colorado Avalanche for their 1995–96 Cup season.

8. Teams from the east (NHA/NHL) and west (PCHA/WCHL/WHL) competed against each other for the Stanley Cup for 13 seasons between 1914 and 1926. On how many occasions did a team from the west successfully capture the Cup?
a) 3   b) 4   c) 5   d) 6

a) 3. The western champions were successful on only three occasions: The Vancouver Millionaires defeated the Ottawa Senators in three straight games in 1915; the Seattle Metropolitans defeated the Montreal Canadiens three games to one in 1917; and the Victoria Cougars defeated the Canadiens three games to one in 1925. The NHA/NHL teams were triumphant on nine occasions, and in 1919 there was no winner declared when the finals between the Canadiens and Seattle were canceled after five games due to the influenza epidemic.

9. When was the Stanley Cup first won in April?
a) 1920   b) 1922   c) 1924   d) 1926

a) 1920. The Ottawa Senators defeated the Seattle Metropolitans 6–1 on April 1, 1920, in the fifth and deciding game, which had been relocated from Ottawa to Toronto. Poor ice conditions had caused problems in the first three games, so the last two were moved to artificial ice. This marked the first year that the final Stanley Cup game was played in April. The following year, the fifth and deciding game was played on April 4, but the playoffs weren't played in April again until 1926, when three of four games between the Montreal Maroons and Victoria Cougars took place in that month.

10. Where was the first Stanley Cup final game on artificial ice?
a) Montreal   b) Toronto   c) Vancouver   d) Victoria

b) Toronto. The first Stanley Cup final game to be played on artificial ice took place on March 14, 1914, when the visiting Victoria Aristocrats were defeated 5–2 by the hometown Toronto Blueshirts. Toronto went on to sweep the finals in three straight games. While both Victoria and Vancouver had artificial ice at the time, neither hosted Stanley Cup finals until 1915, when the Ottawa Senators visited Vancouver and played the three-game series on artificial ice.

11. Which of the following future Hall of Famers led the PCHA in scoring in its inaugural season of 1911–12?
a) Tom Dunderdale   b) Harry Hyland
c) Newsy Lalonde   d) Frank Patrick

   c) Newsy Lalonde led the PCHA in scoring in 1911–12 as a member of the Vancouver Millionaires. It was his only season in the PCHA—he returned to the Montreal Canadiens for 1912–13—but he did play for Saskatoon in the WCHL/WHL in the final four years of that league's existence.

PCHA Scoring Leaders, 1911–12

Player	Club	GP	G
Newsy Lalonde	Vancouver	15	27
Harry Hyland	New Westminster	15	26
Tom Dunderdale	Victoria	16	24
Frank Patrick	Vancouver	15	23

12. The Vezina Trophy was first awarded for the 1926–27 season, in memory of the Habs' outstanding goaltender, who had died in March 1926. The Vezina Trophy was presented to the goalie(s) on the team allowing the fewest goals-against during the regular season until the end of the 1981–82 season. Who would have won the most Vezina awards in the nine NHL seasons before it was presented?
a) Clint Benedict   b) Alex Connell
c) Jake Forbes   d) Georges Vezina

   a) Clint Benedict of the Ottawa Senators would have been awarded the Vezina Trophy in five consecutive seasons, from 1918–19 through 1922–23, if it had been presented then.

Best NHL Goals-against Averages

Season	Goalie	Team	GAA
1917–18	Georges Vezina	Montreal Canadiens	3.93
1918–19	Clint Benedict	Ottawa Senators	2.76
1919–20	Clint Benedict	Ottawa Senators	2.66
1920–21	Clint Benedict	Ottawa Senators	3.08
1921–22	Clint Benedict	Ottawa Senators	3.34
1922–23	Clint Benedict	Ottawa Senators	2.18
1923–24	Georges Vezina	Montreal Canadiens	1.97
1924–25	Georges Vezina	Montreal Canadiens	1.81
1925–26	Alex Connell	Ottawa Senators	1.12

13. Who recorded the most goals in a single season in the PCHA?
a) Frank Fredrickson   b) Bernie Morris
c) Gordon Roberts   d) Cyclone Taylor

   c) Dr. Gordon Roberts recorded 43 goals in 23 games with the Vancouver Millionaires in his first season in the PCHA, 1916–17, to establish the all-time single-season scoring record in the league. Roberts was an outstanding left winger who played briefly with the Stanley Cup champion Ottawa Senators in 1909–1910 before he left to study medicine at McGill and play with the Montreal Wanderers in the NHA. He graduated in 1916 and headed to Vancouver to practise medicine and also signed up with the Millionaires. The season after his record 43 goals, his medical career took him to Seattle, where he signed with the Metropolitans of the PCHA. After sitting out one year, he played his final season of professional hockey with the Vancouver Millionaires in 1919–20.

14. Which team won the highest number of league championships in the 13 years of the PCHA?
a) New Westminster   b) Seattle
c) Vancouver   d) Victoria

   c) Vancouver won the PCHA championship six times.
   PCHA champions: 1911–12, New Westminster Royals; 1912–13, Victoria Aristocrats; 1913–14, Victoria Aristocrats; 1914–15, Vancouver Millionaires; 1915–16, Portland Rosebuds; 1916–17, Seattle Metropolitans; 1917–18, Vancouver Millionaires; 1918–19, Seattle Metropolitans; 1919–20, Seattle Metropolitans; 1920–21, Vancouver Millionaires; 1921–22, Vancouver Millionaires; 1922–23, Vancouver Maroons; and 1923–24, Vancouver Maroons. Vancouver and Victoria joined the WCHL in 1924–25 and the league became the WHL for the 1925–26 season. The Victoria Cougars were the league champions in both of these final two seasons of elite professional hockey in the west.

15. For the first four seasons of the NHL, overtime was played until a winner was decided in all regular-season games that were tied after 60 minutes. The NHL began limiting overtime to 20 minutes for the 1921–22 season. Since then, how often have there been no tied games in an entire NHL season?
   a) 0   b) 1   c) 2   d) 3

b) 1. Not one of the NHL's 48 regular-season games ended in a tie during the 1923–24 season.

16. The famed Ottawa Silver Seven dominated Stanley Cup play between 1903 and 1906. Many different players moved in and out of the Silver Seven lineup during these years. How many players from the Ottawa Silver Seven have been inducted into the Hockey Hall of Fame?
a) 5   b) 6   c) 7   d) 8

  d) 8. The eight Hall of Fame members who played for the Ottawa Silver Seven are Billy Gilmour, Bouse Hutton, Percy LeSueur, Frank McGee, Harvey Pulford, Alf Smith, Tommy Smith and Harry Westwick.

17. How many Hall of Famers played with the Montreal Maroons at some time during their NHL career?
a) 10   b) 11   c) 12   d) 13

  c) 12. The following Hall of Famers all skated with the Montreal Maroons at some point between 1924 and 1938: Clint Benedict, Toe Blake, George Boucher, Punch Broadbent, Lionel Conacher, Alex Connell, Red Dutton, Reg Noble, Babe Siebert, Hooley Smith, Nels Stewart and Carl Voss.

18. How many NHL franchises have been located in Montreal?
a) 2   b) 3   c) 4   d) 5

  b) 3. The Montreal Canadiens and the Montreal Wanderers were charter members of the NHL in 1917–18, but the Wanderers had played only four NHL games when they dropped out of the league after their arena was destroyed by fire. The Montreal Maroons competed in the NHL from 1924–25 to the end of the 1937–38 season.

19. How many nations competed in the hockey tournament at the 1920 Olympics?
a) 4   b) 7   c) 8   d) 10

  b) 7. Belgium, Canada, Czechoslovakia, France, Sweden, Switzerland and the United States all competed in the first hockey tournament held at an Olympic Games.

20. Who was the last player to score a Stanley Cup playoff goal while playing for a non-NHL team?
a) Frank Fredrickson   b) Frank Foyston
c) Harry Meeking   d) Jack Walker

a) Frank Fredrickson scored the third goal for the Victoria Cougars in a 3–2 win over the Montreal Maroons on April 3, 1926. Three days later, the Maroons went on to defeat the Cougars 2–0 to capture the Cup in the last series for the trophy that involved a non-NHL team.

Third Period: Expert Trivia

1. Name the first American-based hockey team to play in the Stanley Cup finals.

The Portland Rosebuds lost the Stanley Cup finals to the Montreal Canadiens in 1916. The following year, the Seattle Mets won against Montreal.

2. What was the result of the first series between the PCHA and the NHA (the forerunner of the NHL)?

The first series was held in 1913, when the Victoria Aristocrats defeated the Quebec Bulldogs in two out of three. (Victoria won game one 7–5, Quebec game two 6–3 and Victoria game three 6–1.) Quebec was the Stanley Cup champion at the time but wasn't willing to put up the Cup as a prize, so the challenge was an exhibition series. The following year, it was agreed that the winners of the two leagues would play off for the Cup. This time, the Victoria Aristocrats were again champions of the PCHA and traveled to Toronto to play the NHA-winning Blueshirts and Toronto swept the series by scores of 5–2, 6–5 (in overtime) and 2–1.

3. Since 1893, what is the only year no Stanley Cup winner was declared?

In 1919, an epidemic of Spanish influenza was sweeping North America and hit Seattle at the same time as the Stanley Cup finals between the Montreal Canadiens and the Seattle Metropolitans. Several players fell ill, so the series was canceled with two wins for each team and one tie. In fact, the Canadiens' Joe Hall was hospitalized for the flu in Seattle and died a few days after the cancellation.

4. What was the first time brothers faced each other in a Stanley Cup final series?

Two sets of brothers faced each other in the 1923 Cup finals between the Ottawa Senators and Vancouver Maroons. Cy Denneny faced off for Ottawa while his brother Corb played for Vancouver and George Boucher played for Ottawa while his brother Frank played for Vancouver.

5. Name the only NHL franchise to play out of one city for at least five NHL seasons and never participate in a playoff game during its entire stay in that city.

The Hamilton Tigers from 1920–21 to 1924–25. The NHL franchise in Quebec relocated to Hamilton for 1920–21 and the team suffered through four losing seasons. In their fifth, 1924–25, the team had an impressive winning record of 19–10–1 and finished first in the NHL, but the schedule had been expanded by six games and the Tigers felt they were entitled to an additional $200 each for the extra games and the playoffs. Players were suspended and fined, and Hamilton was disqualified from the playoffs. The team was eventually sold and became the New York Americans for the 1925–26 season, and Hamilton is still waiting to get another taste of NHL hockey, let alone qualify for a playoff game.

6. Has a university-based hockey team ever won the Stanley Cup?

No. Queen's University, located in Kingston, Ontario, unsuccessfully challenged for the Stanley Cup on three different occasions, but no university-based hockey team has ever won the Cup. Queen's lost their first challenge 5–1 against the Montreal AAA on March 9, 1895. Their second was a 6–2 loss to the Montreal Shamrocks on March 14, 1899. Their third unsuccessful attempt was a two-game series where they lost 16–7 and 12–7 to the Ottawa Silver Seven on February 27 and 28, 1906.

7. What was the first hockey team called the Maple Leafs to challenge for the Stanley Cup?

The Winnipeg Maple Leafs unsuccessfully challenged the Montreal Wanderers for the Stanley Cup in 1908. The Wanderers defeated these Leafs by scores of 11–5 and 9–3 in games held on March 10 and 12 in Montreal.

8. The NHL opened its first season with two games on December 19, 1917. Who won those first two games?

The Montreal Canadiens and the Montreal Wanderers. The Canadiens defeated the Ottawa Senators by a score of 7–4 and went on to countless wins in the league. The Wanderers defeated the Toronto Arenas 10–9, but that was their lone NHL victory. The Wanderers played three more games—an 11–2 loss to the Canadiens on December 22, a 6–3 loss to Ottawa on December 26 and a 9–2 loss to Ottawa on December 29—but on January 2, 1918, the Montreal Arena burned down, leaving the Canadiens and the Wanderers without a rink. While the

Canadiens relocated to the Jubilee rink, the Wanderers decided to withdraw for the season and never did return to the NHL. Both the Canadiens and the Toronto Arenas were awarded a defaulted Wanderers game to balance the schedule, so the Wanderers' NHL record shows one win and five losses, when in fact they only played four games in the league.

9. What was the last Maritime Canadian team to challenge for the Stanley Cup?

The Sydney Miners were the champions of the Maritime Professional Hockey League and challenged the Quebec Bulldogs for the Cup at the end of the 1912–13 season. The Miners traveled to Quebec, where the Bulldogs easily defeated them by scores of 14–3 on March 8 and 6–2 on March 10.

10. Beginning in 1909–1910, the NHA existed for eight seasons, until most of the teams were transferred to the NHL for the 1917–18 season. In the first season of the NHA, there were seven teams. Three were based in Montreal, one in Ottawa and three in small Ontario towns. Name the three Ontario towns that had NHA franchises in its first season of operation.

Cobalt and Haileybury were in northern Ontario's mining district and stayed in the NHA for only one season. Renfrew played in the league for a second and final season in 1910–11.

11. What were the names of the three Montreal teams that operated in the first season of the NHA?

The Canadiens, the Shamrocks and the Wanderers. The Shamrocks and the Wanderers were both established teams that shifted over from other leagues and the Canadiens were in their first season of operation in 1909–10.

12. Name the only team to lose four consecutive Stanley Cup final series.

The Vancouver franchise of the PCHA lost in four consecutive Stanley Cup finals between 1921 and 1924. Known as the Millionaires in the first two, they lost to the Ottawa Senators in five games in 1921 and to the Toronto St. Pats in five in 1922. The franchise changed its name to the Maroons for the 1922–23 season and lost the finals in both 1923 and 1924. In a three-team final series, Vancouver represented the PCHA and was eliminated by the Ottawa Senators in 1923 and the Montreal Canadiens in 1924. In both cases, the teams from the east went on to defeat the WCHL champions for the Cup.

13. The demise of the Western Hockey League at the end of the 1925–26 season allowed the NHL to take control as the only major professional hockey league in North America. Name the six teams that closed out the last season of the WHL.

The Calgary Tigers, Edmonton Eskimos, Portland Rosebuds, Saskatoon Crescents, Vancouver Maroons and Victoria Cougars were the six teams to play in the final season of the WHL. While the Edmonton Eskimos finished in first place, it was the third-place Victoria Cougars who represented the league in the Stanley Cup finals in the last competition between the NHL and a rival league for the Stanley Cup. The Montreal Maroons defeated the Cougars three games to one in these last finals that included a non-NHL team.

14. What was the first Canadian-based professional hockey league?

The Ontario Professional Hockey League, also known as the "Trolley League," operated for four seasons between 1907 and 1911. It was at its largest with six franchises in 1908–09, and teams were located in Brantford, Berlin (Kitchener), Galt, Guelph, Toronto, St. Catharines and Waterloo at various times throughout the four-year history of the league. The league was represented in Stanley Cup challenges on four occasions, none of which were successful. Toronto was defeated 6–4 by the Montreal Wanderers in a challenge game on March 14, 1908. Galt was defeated by the Ottawa Senators 12–3 and 3–1 in a two-game total-goals series played in January 1910. The Montreal Wanderers defeated Berlin (Kitchener) 7–3 in a March 12, 1910, challenge, and Galt was defeated by the Ottawa Senators 7–4 on March 13 in the final season of the league's existence. But the International Professional Hockey League, with four American and one Canadian franchise, had actually been the first professional hockey league, beginning in 1904. The Sault Ste. Marie Marlboroughs of the International Pro Hockey League were the first Canadian-based professional hockey team. But the league was largely based in northern Michigan with teams located in Calumet-Larium, Sault Ste. Marie (Michigan and Ontario), Pittsburgh and Houghton. This league only survived for three seasons and finished playing in 1907.

15. Name the only player to lead the NHL in goals and points in his rookie season.

Nels Stewart had an outstanding rookie season with the Montreal Maroons in 1925–26 when he scored a league-leading 34 goals and 42 points in 36 games. He then scored a series-leading six goals in a four-game final series against the Victoria Cougars to lead the Maroons to their first Stanley Cup victory in their second NHL season. He went on to star with the Maroons, Boston Bruins and New York Americans until his retirement after the 1939–40 season. He was elected to the Hockey Hall of Fame in 1962.

16. Name the only player to win an NHL award while representing Hamilton's franchise in the NHL.

Billy Burch won the Hart Trophy as the NHL's most valuable player as a member of the Hamilton Tigers in 1924–25, the last season the franchise spent in that city.

17. The Ottawa Senators won three Stanley Cups in four seasons from 1919–20 to 1922–23. One player was a future Hall of Famer who suited up for the Stanley Cup champions of 1920 and 1921 before retiring for the 1921–22 season but changed his mind and was on the 1923 Cup winner as well. Can you name him?

Jack Darragh was a well-established veteran by the time he was a member of the Cup-winning teams of 1920, 1921 and 1923. He won his first Cup in 1911 with the Ottawa Senators, then of the NHA. He played his final NHL season in 1923–24, as he died of a ruptured appendix in June 1924. Darragh was inducted into the Hockey Hall of Fame in 1962.

18. What happened in the first Stanley Cup playoff scheduled as a best-of-three series?

The first best-of-three Stanley Cup playoffs took place in December 1897. The Montreal Victorias defeated the visiting Ottawa Capitals by a score of 14–2 in a game played on December 27, but the trustees of the Cup felt the teams were unevenly matched and ended the series after that game.

19. Name the three teams who were not Stanley Cup winners but still have their names on the Cup.

The 1914–15 Ottawa Senators, the 1915–16 Portland Rosebuds and the 1917–18 Vancouver Millionaires all eliminated the defending Cup champions in their own league and added their names to the trophy. However, they were unable to capture the Cup in the NHA/NHL-PCHA finals and were not true Stanley Cup champions.

20. Name the only player known to have played all six positions in one Stanley Cup playoff game.

King Clancy played all six positions in the Ottawa Senators' Cup-clinching 1–0 victory over the Edmonton Eskimos on March 31, 1923. Clancy replaced Ottawa netminder Clint Benedict for two minutes while the goaltender served a minor penalty.

Overtime: Four on Four

1. The last time the NHL was comprised of four teams was in 1923–24. Name the four clubs that competed in the NHL during that season.

The Hamilton Tigers, Montreal Canadiens, Ottawa Senators and Toronto St. Pats were the four teams that competed in the NHL in 1923–24. The NHL added two franchises (the Boston Bruins and Montreal Maroons) for 1924–25.

2. Name the first family of four brothers to play in the NHL.
The Bouchers.

	Season(s)	*Team(s)*
Billy	1921–22 to 1927–28	Canadiens, Bruins, Americans
Bobby	1923–24	Canadiens
Frank	1921–22, 1926–27 to 1937–38, 1943–44	Senators, Rangers
George	1917–18 to 1931–32	Senators, Maroons, Black Hawks

3. A third elite professional hockey league was formed in the west for the 1921–22 season. Name the four teams that competed in the WCHL during that season.

Western Canada Hockey League, 1921–22

Team	W	L	PTS
The Edmonton Eskimos	15	9	30
The Regina Capitals*	14	10	28
The Calgary Tigers	14	10	28
The Saskatoon-Moose Jaw Sheiks	5	19	10

*Playoff champion

4. Name the four times that the Stanley Cup has been won on a neutral ice site.

In 1907, the Montreal Wanderers defeated the Kenora Thistles in a two-game final series, both of which were played in Winnipeg because of poor ice conditions in Kenora.

In 1920, Ottawa defeated Seattle three games to two in the Stanley Cup finals. Both games four and five were moved from Ottawa to Toronto, again because of poor ice conditions, and were played on the artificial ice at Toronto's Mutual Street Arena.

In 1923, Ottawa defeated Edmonton two games to none and both were played in Vancouver. Ottawa had previously defeated Vancouver, who were champions of the PCHA, and by winning that series advanced to play Edmonton.

In 1924, the Montreal Canadiens defeated the Calgary Tigers in two straight. The second—and Cup-winning—game was moved to artificial ice in Ottawa because the ice in Montreal was poor.

Game 3: One League

1926 to 1955

The Western Hockey League folded at the end of the 1925–26 season and left the NHL with no rival as the elite professional hockey league. It expanded from seven to 10 teams in 1926–27, adding the Detroit Cougars, the Chicago Black Hawks and the New York Rangers, and while the Depression and World War II saw the NHL shrink back to six teams by 1942–43, the era of the Original Six (which lasted until 1966–67) is fondly remembered by older hockey fans. And the postwar period saw tremendous growth in the game and the introduction of hockey to television, including the first broadcast of *Hockey Night in Canada* in 1952.

First Period: Who Am I?

1. As a member of the 1939 Boston Bruins, I scored three overtime goals in one playoff series against the New York Rangers.

Mel Hill acquired the nickname "Sudden Death" with his overtime winners in games one, two and seven of the 1939 semifinals.

2. I was the losing coach of one NHL franchise in the Stanley Cup finals one year but coached another team to the Cup the next year.

Dick Irvin was the losing coach when Montreal defeated Chicago three games to two in 1931, but he turned the tables in the 1932 Cup finals in which Toronto defeated the New York Rangers in three straight games.

3. I won the Hart Trophy four times in the 1930s.
Eddie Shore of the Boston Bruins won the Hart Trophy as the NHL's most valuable player in 1933, 1935, 1936 and 1938.

4. I recorded an amazing 22 shutouts in 44 games.
George Hainsworth recorded 22 shutouts while playing in all 44 regular-season games with the 1928–29 Montreal Canadiens and had a 0.92 goals-against-average as he captured the Vezina Trophy for a third consecutive season.

5. I was the first NHL player to record 50 or more points in an NHL season.
Howie Morenz of the Montreal Canadiens recorded 51 points (33–18–51) in the 1927–28 season.

6. I played goal for Chicago in all 44 games in their first season in the NHL (1926–27). In the second season, I retired from goaltending—only to become the Black Hawks' coach for the second half of the season.
Hugh Lehman had a 19–22–3 record and 2.49 goals-against average for the Hawks in 1926–27 and played in four games in 1927–28 before taking the coaching duties over from Barney Stanley. As a coach with a 3–17–1 record Lehman had little success with the struggling team, however.

7. I played my last game in the NHL—and my Hall of Fame playing career—as a member of the 1927 Cup-winning Ottawa Senators and relocated as coach and general manager of the Detroit Cougars for the following season.
Jack Adams' Hall of Fame career included two Stanley Cup championships as a player: as a member of the 1918 Toronto Arenas and the 1927 Ottawa Senators. Adams relocated to Detroit as coach and GM in 1927–28 and remained there as GM until the end of the 1961–62 season—a tenure that included seven more Stanley Cup championships.

8. When Toronto traded five regulars—Bob Goldham, Ernie Dickens, Bud Poile, Gus Bodnar and Gaye Stewart—to Chicago in November 1947 to obtain scoring star Max Bentley, I came to Toronto with Max in the deal.
Cy Thomas played six games for Chicago and eight games for Toronto in 1947–48, his only year in the NHL.

9. I was on two Cup winners with the Toronto Maple Leafs, following in the footsteps of my father, who was on two Cup winners with the Ottawa Senators in the 1920s.

Fleming MacKell was on Cup winners in 1948–49 and 1950–51. His father, Jack MacKell, had been on the Ottawa Senators in 1919–20 and 1920–21.

10. I won the Lady Byng Trophy as a defenseman in 1949.

Bill Quackenbush played in all 60 games of the Detroit Red Wings' 1948–49 season and didn't receive a single penalty. He was traded to Boston after that season.

11. I won the Art Ross Trophy and played my only NHL All–Star Game in 1949.

Roy Conacher won the scoring race as a member of the Chicago Black Hawks, totaling 68 points in 60 games in 1948–49, and was named to the First All–Star Team.

12. My final six NHL seasons were spent with the Detroit Red Wings, where I won three Stanley Cup championships.

Bob Goldham was traded to Detroit by Chicago in July 1950. He played for the Red Wings from 1950 to 1956 and won the Cup in 1952, 1954 and 1955.

13. I am the first defenseman to score 20 goals in a single NHL season.

Flash Hollett recorded 20 goals in 50 games with the 1944–45 Detroit Red Wings.

14. I was the last active player in the NHL who played with the New York/Brooklyn Americans.

Ken Mosdell played 41 games for the 1941–42 Brooklyn Americans and was the last active member of that franchise in the NHL when he played three playoff games for the Montreal Canadiens in the 1959 Stanley Cup playoffs.

15. I played for the four American franchises of the Original Six during my six NHL seasons. My biggest moment came when I scored the Cup-winning goal in the 1950 finals against the New York Rangers.

Pete Babando scored the Cup-winning goal in the second overtime period of game seven against the New York Rangers in the 1950 finals.

16. Three of my brothers proceeded me as Stanley Cup champions.

Frank Boucher won the Cup as a member of the 1927–28 New York Rangers. George Boucher had been on the Cup-winning Ottawa Senators in 1920, 1921, 1923 and 1927, while Billy and Bobby Boucher had both been members of the 1924 Montreal Canadiens. Frank Boucher won a second Cup skating with the New York Rangers in 1933.

17. I was a rookie teammate of eight-year NHL veteran Gordie Howe when the Detroit Red Wings won the Stanley Cup in 1953–54. Twenty years later, I was the head coach in Gordie's first WHA season as we captured the Avco Cup Trophy as playoff champions of the league.

Bill Dineen played a total of five seasons in the NHL. In his first two, 1953–54 and 1954–55, the Red Wings won the Stanley Cup. When Gordie Howe went to the WHA as a member of the Houston Aeros in 1973–74, Dineen was his head coach when the Aeros won the league championship for two consecutive years, 1974 and 1975.

18. I was the last individual to lead the NHL season scoring race while I was playing on a last-place team.

Max Bentley recorded 72 points in 60 games as the leading scorer in 1946–47 playing with the sixth-place Black Hawks.

19. I am the only NHL player to become president of the league.

Mervyn "Red" Dutton played for the Calgary Tigers in the PCHA/WCHL/WHL from 1921 until the demise of the league in 1926. Dutton went on to play in 10 NHL seasons, the first four with the Montreal Maroons and the last six with the New York Americans, and stayed on with the Americans as coach and general manager through the end of the 1941–42 season, the last in the NHL for this franchise (by then renamed the Brooklyn Americans). He was named NHL president to replace Frank Calder, who died in 1943, and remained president until Clarence Campbell succeeded him. Dutton was inducted into the Hockey Hall of Fame in 1958.

20. I won both the Lady Byng and the Hart in 1948.
   Buddy O'Connor won the Lady Byng and the Hart awards in 1948 as a member of the New York Rangers. He had been traded to New York by Montreal in August 1947.

Second Period: Multiple Choice

1. Which of the 1926–27 expansion teams had the best record in their first NHL season?
a) The Chicago Black Hawks   b) The Detroit Cougars
c) The New York Rangers
   c) The New York Rangers. All three teams were in the American Division, where New York finished first with a 25–13–6 record, Chicago third with 19–22–3 and Detroit fifth and last with 12–28–4.

2. In which season did NHL teams begin playing a 70-game schedule?
a) 1942–43   b) 1945–46   c) 1946–47   d) 1949–50
   d) 1949–50. The NHL schedule included 50 games per team in 1942–43 and 1945–46 and grew to 60 in 1946–47, then to 70 in 1949–50.

3. Each of the following forwards became NHL legends because of their contributions after their playing days were over. However, all four were inducted into the Hockey Hall of Fame as players. Which of them played the most games in the National Hockey League?
a) Jack Adams   b) Dick Irvin
c) Lester Patrick   d) Art Ross
   a) Jack Adams played a total of 173 games. Dick Irvin had 94 games for the Chicago Black Hawks, while Art Ross had three NHL games and GM-coach Lester Patrick had two, one in 1926–27 on defense and one in the 1928 Stanley Cup finals—as an emergency replacement for his injured goalie Lorne Chabot.

4. How many Hockey Hall of Fame inductees finished their NHL playing careers with the New York/Brooklyn Americans?
a) 12   b) 13   c) 14   d) 15

b) 13. The following all played their last NHL game with the New York Americans: Punch Broadbent, Charlie Conacher, Hap Day, Red Dutton, Wilf "Shorty" Green, Ching Johnson, Newsy Lalonde, Harry Oliver, "Bullet" Joe Simpson, Eddie Shore, Hooley Smith, Nels Stewart and Roy Worters.

5. Which team had the most consecutive first-place finishes in the Original Six era?
a) Boston   b) Detroit   c) Montreal   d) Toronto

b) Detroit had seven consecutive first-place finishes from 1948–49 to 1954–55.

6. The Toronto Maple Leafs had three consecutive Calder Trophy winners in the 1940s. Which of these players was not included in this sweep of the rookie of the year award?
a) Gaye Stewart   b) Gus Bodnar
c) Frank McCool   d) Howie Meeker

d) Howie Meeker. He did win the rookie of the year award in 1947, but he wasn't one of the three consecutive winners. Gaye Stewart won in 1943, Gus Bodnar in 1944, Frank McCool in 1945, Edgar Laprade took it to New York in 1946 and Meeker brought it back to Toronto the next year.

7. The following players had lengthy NHL careers in Boston and Detroit. Which player actually began his career somewhere else?
a) Warren Godfrey   b) Bill Quackenbush
c) Vic Stasiuk   d) Johnny Bucyk

c) Vic Stasiuk played in Chicago before going on to Boston and Detroit.

8. Who was the last player to lead the NHL in goals scored while playing for the Toronto Maple Leafs?
a) Syl Apps   b) Max Bentley
c) Ted Kennedy   d) Gaye Stewart

d) Gaye Stewart recorded 37 goals in the 1945–46 season, which was the last time a Maple Leaf has led the league in goal-scoring.

9. Which of the following individuals was selected to the First or Second NHL All–Star Team on the most occasions?
a) Jack Adams   b) Frank Boucher
c) Dick Irvin   d) Lester Patrick

Maurice "Rocket" Richard was a prolific scorer who became the first NHL player to record 50 goals in a season and 500 goals in a career.

c) Dick Irvin. All four were elected to the Hockey Hall of Fame on the basis of their outstanding playing careers, and Boucher was the only one still playing when the NHL began naming an official First and Second All–Star Team at the end of the 1930–31 season. But the selection process included a coach for the first 16 seasons, which explains why Irvin was able to obtain more placings than Boucher.

Irvin was selected to a First or Second Team on nine different occasions as head coach of the Chicago Black Hawks, Toronto Maple Leafs and Montreal Canadiens. Lester Patrick was chosen as the First Team coach on seven occasions, including the first six times an All–Star Team was named. Boucher was named to the All–Star Teams on six different occasions, four times as a player (he was the First Team center for three consecutive seasons from 1932–33 to 1934–35 and the Second Team center for 1930–31) and twice as a coach, 1939–40 with the Second and 1941–42 with the First Team. Jack Adams of the Detroit Red Wings was named to an NHL All–Star Team on three separate occasions, as the First Team coach for 1936–37 and 1942–43 and the Second Team coach for 1944–45.

10. When was the last time that the Stanley Cup was won in March?
a) 1927   b) 1929   c) 1931   d) 1935

b) 1929. The Boston Bruins defeated the New York Rangers 2–1 to win the best-of-three series in two games on March 29, 1929.

11. The Maple Leafs won consecutive Stanley Cups between 1947 and 1949. Which player led Toronto's playoff scoring for all three years?
a) Syl Apps   b) Max Bentley
c) Ted Kennedy   d) Sid Smith

c) Ted Kennedy was an outstanding player for the Leafs, leading the team playoff scoring with nine points in 1947, 14 in 1948 and eight in 1949 (he had also led Leafs scorers with nine points during the 1945 championship). None of the other players listed were members of all three of these Stanley Cup-winning teams. Syl Apps retired after the 1948 championship, and Max Bentley and Sid Smith didn't see their first playoff action as Leafs until 1948.

12. Three NHL All–Star games were played as fundraisers during the 1930s: the Ace Bailey Benefit Game in 1934, the

Howie Morenz Memorial Game in 1937 and the Babe Siebert Memorial Game in 1939. How many players took part in all three?
a) 0   b) 2   c) 4   d) 6

   b) 2. Eddie Shore played for the All–Stars as a representative of the Boston Bruins in all three of these games. Busher Jackson played in the 1934 Ace Bailey Benefit Game as a member of the Toronto Maple Leafs, in the 1937 Howie Morenz Memorial Game representing Toronto on the NHL All–Stars and in the 1939 Babe Siebert Memorial Game representing the New York Americans on the NHL All–Stars.

13. How many regular-season overtime games were played in the 25 seasons of the Original Six era, from 1942 to 1967?
a) 0   b) 3   c) 9   d) 27

   b) 3. The NHL had introduced a 10-minute non-sudden-death period to be played following regulation-time ties in 1928–29 and this rule was in effect until November 21, 1942, when the league discontinued all overtime play in regular-season games because it was hard to schedule trains during the war. The only three regular-season overtime games played in the Original Six era took place before this point in the 1942–43 season.

   NHL Regular-Season Overtime Games: November 7, 1942, Montreal Canadiens 3, New York Rangers 4; November 8, 1942, Chicago Black Hawks 3, Detroit Red Wings 3; November 10, 1942, Chicago Black Hawks 3, New York Rangers 5.

14. Who holds the career record for most points as a Montreal Maroon?
a) Babe Siebert   b) Hooley Smith
c) Nels Stewart   d) Jimmy Ward

   b) Hooley Smith is the all-time career leader with 281 points in 387 games over nine seasons with the Montreal Maroons. Reginald "Hooley" Smith had an outstanding 17-year career in the NHL that included stops in Ottawa, Boston and New York (with the Americans), but his best hockey was played as a member of the Maroons' S-Line where he teamed with Siebert and Stewart. Smith earned two NHL All–Star Team selections and was a 1935 Stanley Cup champion Maroon. He was inducted into the Hockey Hall of Fame in 1972.

15. Who was the NHL's leading scorer in 1926–27? (Hint: He led the Western Hockey League in scoring in its final season of 1925–26.)
a) Frank Boucher   b) Bill Cook
c) Frank Fredrickson   d) Dick Irvin

b) Bill Cook led the WHL in scoring with 31 goals and 13 assists for 44 points in 30 games as a member of the Saskatoon Crescents in the 1925–26 season. When the league folded, he signed with the New York Rangers for their first season (1926–27) and led the NHL in scoring. Boucher, Cook, Fredrickson and Irvin had all finished in the top 10 in scoring in 1925–26 in the WHL and the four continued the trend in the NHL the next season.

NHL Scoring Leaders, 1926–27

		GP	G	A	PTS
Bill Cook	New York Rangers	44	33	4	37
Dick Irvin	Chicago	43	18	18	36
Howie Morenz	Montreal Canadiens	44	25	7	32
Frank Fredrickson	Detroit, Boston	41	18	13	31
Babe Dye	Chicago	41	25	5	30
Ace Bailey	Toronto	42	15	13	28
Frank Boucher	New York Rangers	44	13	15	28

16. Name the only player to win the Vezina Trophy and serve as captain in the same NHL season.
a) Turk Broda   b) Bill Durnan
c) Charlie Gardiner   d) Tiny Thompson

c) Charlie Gardiner served as the captain of the Stanley Cup champion Chicago Black Hawks and won the Vezina Trophy in his final NHL season in 1933–34. While Durnan served as captain of the Montreal Canadiens for the last part of the 1947–48 season, Turk Broda was awarded the Vezina Trophy. And neither Broda nor Thompson ever served as captains of their respective teams.

17. How many times has a Stanley Cup final series been played in more than two cities?
a) 0   b) 1   c) 2   d) 3

b) 1. The 1932 Stanley Cup finals were played in three different cities. The New York Rangers were left without a home rink when the circus took over Madison Square Garden after game one.

1932 Stanley Cup Finals

April 5	New York	Toronto 6, New York Rangers 4
April 7	Boston	Toronto 6, New York Rangers 2
April 9	Toronto	Toronto 6, New York Rangers 4

(Toronto won the best-of-five series three games to none.)

18. When was the last time the Stanley Cup playoffs included a two-game total-goals series?
a) 1926   b) 1931   c) 1936   d) 1941

c) 1936. Two quarterfinals were decided by the two-game total-goals format during the 1936 Stanley Cup playoffs. The quarterfinals were changed to best-of-three affairs for 1937.

1936 Stanley Cup Quarterfinals

| Series B | March 24 | Toronto 0 at Boston 3 |
| | March 26 | Boston 3 at Toronto 8 |

(Toronto won the total-goals series eight goals to six.)

| Series C | March 24 | Chicago 0 at New York Americans 3 |
| | March 26 | New York Americans 4 at Chicago 5 |

(The New York Americans won the total-goals series by seven goals to five.)

19. Which player led the NHL in penalty minutes for a record eight consecutive seasons?
a) Sprague Cleghorn   b) Bill Ezinicki
c) Red Horner   d) Eddie Shore

c) Red Horner was a Leaf when he led the league in penalty minutes for eight consecutive seasons from 1932–33 to 1939–40, his last in the NHL.

20. Which team was the first to lose 40 games in an NHL season?
a) The Chicago Black Hawks   b) The New York Americans
c) The New York Rangers   d) The Philadelphia Quakers

a) The Chicago Black Hawks lost 47 games in 1950–51. They had come close the previous season, when the NHL schedule had expanded to 70 games per team and the Hawks recorded 38 losses. And the 1943–44 New York Rangers had managed to lose 39 of 50 games. While the Americans had struggled through most of their existence, their season high was 29 losses (which they reached in four different seasons). The Philadelphia Quakers had lost 36 of their 44 games in 1930–31 and didn't achieve 40 losses largely because there were only 44 games that season.

Third Period: Expert Trivia

1. Which U.S.-based team was placed in an unusual division during the NHL expansion in the 1920s?

The New York Americans actually played in the Canadian Division from 1926 to 1938. In 1926–27, when the NHL expanded to 10 teams, there were six American- and four Canadian-based teams and the Amerks were placed in the Canadian Division along with Toronto, Ottawa and the two Montreal teams.

2. In what season did the first all-American Stanley Cup finals take place?

In 1929, the Boston Bruins defeated the New York Rangers two games to none.

3. When did the Brooklyn (formerly New York) Americans play their last NHL game?

On Tuesday March 17, 1942, the Brooklyn Americans lost to the Bruins 8–3 in the Boston Garden.

4. Name the two players whose single NHL game was a playoff appearance for the 1950 Cup-winning Detroit Red Wings.

Gord Haidy played a single game during the semifinals against the Toronto Maple Leafs and Doug McKay played one in the finals against the New York Rangers.

5. The Detroit franchise was known as the Cougars from 1927 to 1930, the Falcons from 1930 to 1932 and the Red Wings from then on. Name the five players who have played for Detroit as Cougars, Falcons and Red Wings.

Larry Aurie, Ebbie Goodfellow, George Hay, Herbie Lewis and Reg Noble.

6. Vic Lynn is recognized as the only player to suit up for all of the Original Six NHL teams. Name the four players who played for five of the Original Six from 1942 to 1967.

Harry Lumley and Bud Poile played for all of the Original Six teams except Montreal, Gaye Stewart played for all except Boston and Bronco Horvath played for all except Detroit.

7. Name the two brothers who were teammates in four different NHL cities.

Des and Earl Roche were teammates on the Montreal Maroons in 1932–33, the Ottawa Senators in 1933–34, the St. Louis Eagles in 1934–35 and later that season the Detroit Red Wings. They also played together on numerous minor-league teams.

8. Henri and Maurice Richard played a total of 2,234 regular-season games between them, all for the Montreal Canadiens. Name the five other pairs of brothers who played a total of more than 500 NHL games combined, but with only one NHL team. (Hint: One pair of brothers did this with Montreal, Toronto or Detroit and two pairs did it with the New York Rangers.)

Neil and Mac Colville combined for 817 games with the New York Rangers; Lynn and Muzz Patrick for 621 games with the New York Rangers; Don and Nick Metz for 690 games with the Toronto Maple Leafs; Mud and Eddie Bruneteau for 591 games with the Detroit Red Wings; and Aurel and Rene Joliat for 656 with the Montreal Canadiens (Aurel played 655 and Rene played in a single game).

9. What was the longest overtime game played in the Original Six era?

Jack McLean scored the winning goal at 10:18 of the fourth overtime period in a semifinal game on March 23, 1943, as Toronto defeated Detroit 3–2. The only other game to go into a fourth overtime period in the Original Six era was a semifinal between Detroit and Montreal on March 27, 1951, when Rocket Richard scored at 1:09 of the fourth overtime period to give Montreal a 3–2 win.

10. Name the captains of the Original Six teams in the first year of the era (1942–43).

The Toronto Maple Leafs, Syl Apps; the Montreal Canadiens, Toe Blake; the New York Rangers, Ott Heller; the Boston Bruins, Dit Clapper; the Chicago Black Hawks, Doug Bentley; and the Detroit Red Wings, Sid Abel.

11. What was the shortest interval between a team's winning the Stanley Cup and either moving or leaving the league?

Three seasons. The Montreal Maroons won the Stanley Cup in 1935 and continued to play in the NHL from 1935–36 through the end of the 1937–38 season, when the franchise ceased operations. The Ottawa Senators won the Cup in 1927 and played for the next four seasons, taking one off in 1931–32 and coming back for two more as the Senators and in 1934–35 as the St. Louis Eagles before that franchise ceased operations. All other Stanley Cup winners to date have continued to play in the city where they won the Cup.

12. Name the first NHL franchise to win the Stanley Cup, miss the playoffs and win the Stanley Cup again, all in three consecutive NHL seasons.

The Toronto Maple Leafs won the Stanley Cup in 1945, missed the Stanley Cup playoffs in 1946 and were repeat champions in 1947. The Detroit Red Wings came close to duplicating the feat. They missed the playoffs in 1935, won the Cup in 1936 and 1937 and missed the playoffs again in 1938. The only NHL team to match the Leafs' record from 1945 through 1947 was the Montreal Canadiens, who won the Stanley Cup in 1969, didn't qualify for the playoffs in 1970 and won the Cup again in 1971.

13. Name the only three brothers in the Hockey Hall of Fame.

Charlie, Lionel and Roy Conacher. While Lionel wasn't inducted until 1994 and Roy until 1998, all of the Conacher brothers had outstanding NHL careers and are highly deserving members of the Hockey Hall of Fame. Right winger Charlie played for the Maple Leafs from 1929 to 1938 and was the leading goal scorer in the NHL on five occasions during that time. He was also a member of the first Toronto team to win the Cup, in 1932. He finished his career with one season with the Detroit Red Wings and two with the New York Americans and finally hung up his skates at the end of the 1940–41 season. He was a member of the First or Second All-Star Team on five occasions and was inducted into the Hockey Hall of Fame in 1961. Lionel played 12 NHL seasons between 1925 and 1937 with the Pittsburgh Pirates, New York Americans, Montreal Maroons and Chicago Black Hawks. He won the Cup with the Hawks in 1934 and with the Maroons in 1935. He was elected a First Team All-Star defenseman for 1933–34 and was selected to the Second All-Star Team twice. Left winger Roy played 11 seasons between 1938 and 1952 (his career was interrupted by the last three years of World War II) for Boston, Detroit and Chicago. He won the Art Ross Trophy and was elected to the First

All-Star Team in 1949 and was on two Cup-winning teams, the 1938–39 and 1940–41 Boston Bruins.

14. These two players both became NHL regulars with the New York Americans in 1934–35, were teammates on the Stanley Cup championship Toronto Maple Leafs in 1941–42 and 1944–45 and closed their careers with the Leafs in 1945–46.

Lorne Carr and Dave "Sweeney" Schriner. While Carr played 14 games for the New York Rangers in 1933–34, he didn't play his first full NHL season until 1934–35 as a member of the New York Americans, putting in seven full seasons before being traded to Toronto prior to the 1941–42 season that brought his first Stanley Cup championship. He played a total of five seasons with the Maple Leafs and retired at the end of the 1945–46 season. Hall of Famer Sweeney Schriner saw his first NHL action in 1934–35 with the Americans and was the NHL's leading scorer in both 1935–36 and 1936–37. He was traded to the Leafs after the 1938–39 season and played for them for six of the next seven seasons, two of them as Cup champions (in 1942 and 1945). Like Carr, he saw his last NHL action at the end of the 1945–46 regular season.

15. Who were the first three brothers to play together on the same NHL club?

Doug, Max and Reg Bentley. While both Doug and Max went on to Hall of Fame careers, brother Reg played only 11 games in the NHL. In 1942–43, he was a member of the Chicago Black Hawks, where he played on the first all-brother forward line in NHL history.

16. While Howie Morenz is synonymous with the Montreal Canadiens of the 1920s and 1930s, he did see NHL action with two other NHL clubs. Can you name them?

The Chicago Black Hawks and the New York Rangers. Howie Morenz was traded to the Hawks by the Canadiens prior to the 1934–35 season and spent one and a half seasons with Chicago before being traded to the Rangers midway through 1935–36. The Rangers traded Morenz back to the Canadiens before the 1936–37 season, and it was during this season that he suffered his career-ending leg injury, six weeks before he died.

17. Most hockey buffs have heard the story of Bill Barilko's last NHL goal, a Stanley Cup winner in sudden-death

overtime on April 21, 1951. Can you name any of the other Leafs who were on the ice when the goal was scored?

The forward line of Cal Gardner, Howie Meeker and Harry Watson, defenseman Bill Juzda and goaltender Al Rollins were the other Toronto players on the ice when Barilko scored his spectacular goal. Meeker and Watson drew assists on the play.

18. When was a sweater numbered 99 first worn in NHL action?

In 1934–35, several of the Montreal Canadiens sported high-double-digit numbers. Both Leo Bourgault and Joe Lamb wore number 99 for the Habs during that season.

19. What was unusual about the game results in the 1927 playoffs?

Six of the 12 playoff games ended in ties. Four ties were allowed to stand in the two-game total-goals series and poor ice ended two games in the finals before a winner was determined.

20. Name the five overtime goal scorers in the 1951 finals between Montreal and Toronto.

Scorer	Game	Time	Score
Sid Smith	Game one, April 11	5:51	Toronto, 3–2
Maurice Richard	Game two, April 14	2:55	Montreal, 3–2
Ted Kennedy	Game three, April 17	4:47	Toronto, 2–1
Harry Watson	Game four, April 19	5:15	Toronto, 3–2
Bill Barilko	Game five, April 21	2:53	Toronto, 3–2

Overtime: Four on Four

1. The NHL began naming a rookie of the year at the end of the 1933–34 season, even though it didn't award the Calder Trophy until 1936–37. Two of those elected in the first six seasons were Russ Blinco of the Montreal Maroons and Syl Apps of the Toronto Maple Leafs and both were Canadian-born. But four of these outstanding rookies were not. Name them.

Mike Karakas, Cully Dahlstrom and Frank Brimsek were all American-born. While Sweeney Schriner was born in Russia, he was raised and learned his hockey in Canada.

Season	Rookie of the Year	Birthplace
1933–34	Russ Blinco, Montreal Maroons	Grand-Mère, Quebec
1934–35	Dave "Sweeney" Schriner, New York Americans	Saratov, Russia
1935–36	Mike Karakas, Chicago Black Hawks	Aurora, Minnesota
1936–37	Syl Apps, Toronto Maple Leafs	Paris, Ontario
1937–38	Cully Dahlstrom, Chicago Black Hawks	Minneapolis, Minnesota
1938–39	Frank Brimsek, Boston Bruins	Eveleth, Minnesota

2. Name the first four defensemen to win the Hart Trophy as the NHL's most valuable player.

The first four defensemen to win the Hart Trophy as the NHL's MVP were: Herb Gardiner (the Montreal Canadiens), 1927; Eddie Shore (the Boston Bruins), 1933; Babe Siebert (the Montreal Canadiens), 1937; Ebbie Goodfellow (the Detroit Red Wings), 1940.

3. Name the four NHL teams that Hall of Famer Babe Siebert suited up for prior to his untimely death in 1939.

Babe Siebert played for the Montreal Maroons from 1926 to 1932, the New York Rangers (1932 to 1934), the Boston Bruins (1933 to 1936) and the Montreal Canadiens from 1936 to 1939.

4. Name the first four captains of the New York Rangers.

The first captain of the New York Rangers was Bill Cook (1926 to 1937), followed by Art Coulter (1937 to 1942), Ott Heller (1942 to 1945) and Neil Colville (1945 to December 21, 1948).

Game 4: A Tale of Two Cities

1955 to 1967

The Montreal Canadiens and Toronto Maple Leafs dominated the last 12 seasons of the Original Six era. The Habs won the Cup seven times and the Leafs four times between 1956 and 1967. Only the Chicago Black Hawks of 1960–61 were able to wrestle the Cup away from them during these years, so it was fitting that Montreal and Toronto faced off for the era's final Stanley Cup championship in Canada's centennial year, 1967.

First Period: Who Am I?

1. I won my fifth and final Stanley Cup as a member of the Chicago Black Hawks in 1961.

Dollard St. Laurent was a member of the Cup-winning Montreal Canadiens in 1953, 1956, 1957 and 1958 but was traded to Chicago in June 1958 and won his final Stanley Cup as a Hawk in 1961.

2. I was traded by the New York Rangers to both the Detroit Red Wings and the Toronto Maple Leafs in 1960.

Eddie Shack was traded to the Detroit Red Wings in February 1960 but didn't have to report when Red Kelly refused to report to New York. In November, the Rangers traded Shack to the Toronto Maple Leafs for Pat Hannigan and Johnny Wilson.

3. I was the second choice overall in the 1966 Amateur Draft and went on to have an outstanding career on defense with three of the Original Six franchises between 1968 and 1985.

Brad Park was chosen second overall in the 1966 Amateur Draft by the New York Rangers and played with the Rangers, Bruins and Red Wings during his NHL career.

4. I didn't miss a game in my entire NHL career, which consisted of nine seasons.

Andy Hebenton played every game from 1955–56 until 1963–64. His first eight seasons were with New York and his last was with Boston—630 consecutive games.

5. I was the only defenseman to take the James Norris Trophy away from Doug Harvey between 1955 through 1962.

Tom Johnson won the Norris Trophy in 1959 for the Montreal Canadiens.

6. I am the only American-born player to be on a Stanley Cup-winning team between 1956 and 1967.

Wayne Hicks was a member of the Chicago Black Hawks in 1960–61, though he played only one regular-season and one playoff game. He was born in Aberdeen, Washington.

7. I was the league leader in assists with 49 in 1959–60 and was awarded the Lady Byng Trophy the same season.

Don McKenney of the Boston Bruins.

8. I was named to the First All-Star Team for five consecutive seasons from 1962–63 to 1966–67.

Pierre Pilote was a First Team All-Star defenseman for five consecutive seasons and won the James Norris Trophy in 1963, 1964 and 1965.

9. I was the first European-trained hockey player to play in the NHL.

Ulf Sterner was a star for the Swedish national team who played four games for the New York Rangers in 1964–65.

10. I was in goal for Bernie Geoffrion's 50th goal in 1961 and Bobby Hull's 51st in 1966.

Cesare Maniago let in Geoffrion's goal as a Leaf in 1961 and Hull's as a Ranger in 1966.

11. I was in goal for the Leafs when they defeated Chicago to win the Stanley Cup in 1962.

Don Simmons had replaced an injured Johnny Bower in game four of the Stanley Cup finals. He finished game four and also played games five and six for Toronto.

12. I captained the Chicago Black Hawks the last time they won the Stanley Cup, in 1961.

Eddie Litzenberger was the captain for Chicago the last time the team won the Cup, in 1961.

13. I was the third Leaf to win the Calder Trophy in the 1960s.

Brit Selby won the Calder Trophy in 1966. He'd been preceded by Dave Keon in 1961 and Kent Douglas in 1963.

14. I was an established NHL defenseman in my fourth season with Detroit when I suffered a career-ending injury in the 1965–66 season.

Doug Barkley was a solid minor-league defenseman who played three games with Chicago in both 1957–58 and 1959–60. His NHL playing career took off after he was traded to the Red Wings in 1962—until it was ended by an eye injury in a 5–1 loss to Chicago on January 30, 1966. He later moved into coaching and was behind the bench for the Red Wings for parts of three different seasons in the 1970s.

15. I remain the last member of the Detroit Red Wings to receive the Art Ross Trophy.

Gordie Howe led the NHL in scoring for the 1962–63 season, marking the last time that a Red Wing has won the Art Ross.

16. I scored the final goal of the Original Six era.

George Armstrong scored the empty-net goal that clinched the Cup at 19:11 of the third period of game six of the 1967 Stanley Cup finals to give Toronto a 3–1 victory.

17. I am the only individual who was head coach of an NHL team when I played in an NHL All–Star Game.

Doug Harvey had taken over as head coach of the New York Rangers for the 1961–62 season when he represented the All–Stars on October 7, 1961, as they defeated Chicago by a score of 3–1.

18. I am the only player who was on a Stanley Cup winner with the Detroit dynasty during the first half of the 1950s as well as the one established by the Montreal Canadiens during the last half of that decade.

Marcel Bonin was a member of the 1954–55 Red Wings and, after stints with the Boston Bruins and the minor-league Quebec Aces, he suited up for the Montreal Canadiens for three consecutive Stanley Cups between 1958 and 1960. His best individual performance came during the 1959 playoffs, when he recorded a league-high 10 goals in 11 games. He was a fascinating character off the ice, too, and had been known to wrestle bears and eat glass.

19. I scored a goal in an NHL All–Star Game but wasn't able to duplicate the feat in regular-season action.

Stan Smrke played a total of nine games for the Montreal Canadiens during the 1956–57 and 1957–58 seasons and recorded no goals and three assists. Still, the Canadiens called Smrke up for the 1957 All–Star Game and he recorded his lone goal as a Canadien at 9:13 of the second period to pull his team ahead 3–2. Unfortunately, the All–Stars added three goals later in the game to defeat the Canadiens by a score of 5–3.

20. I was the first player to appear in 1,000 NHL regular-season games.

Gordie Howe played his 1,000th regular-season game in the NHL on Sunday, November 26, 1961, as the Red Wings were downed 4–1 in Chicago.

Second Period: Multiple Choice

1. Which of the following Hall of Famers played their last game as a Montreal Canadien at the Montreal Forum?
a) Jacques Plante   b) Dickie Moore
c) Bernie Geoffrion   d) Maurice Richard

c) Bernie Geoffrion played his last game as a Montreal Canadien in the 1964 semifinal game seven against the Leafs. Plante, Moore and

Richard all played their last game as a Canadien in Maple Leaf Gardens, Richard in the finals in 1960 and Plante and Moore in the semifinals in 1963.

2. Who recorded the most assists in a single season in the Original Six era?
a) Jean Beliveau   b) Andy Bathgate
c) Stan Mikita   d) Bert Olmstead

   c) Stan Mikita recorded 62 assists in 1966–67. He also recorded 59 in 1964–65 to break the previous record held by Beliveau and Bathgate. Beliveau recorded 58 in 1960–61 and Bathgate recorded 58 in 1963–64 in a split season between New York and Toronto. Olmstead's highest record was 56 in 1955–56.

3. Who was the leading point-getter among defensemen for the 1966–67 season?
a) Gary Bergman   b) Harry Howell
c) Bobby Orr   d) Pierre Pilote

   d) Pierre Pilote.

Leading Scorers among Defensemen for 1966–67

	GP	G	A	PTS
Pierre Pilote, Chicago	70	6	46	52
Bobby Orr, Boston	61	13	28	41
Harry Howell, New York	70	12	28	40
Gary Bergman, Detroit	70	5	30	35
J. C. Tremblay, Montreal	60	8	26	34
Pat Stapleton, Chicago	70	3	31	34

4. Many fans identify the following four defensemen with the Leafs of the early 1960s. Which one made his final appearance as a Leaf at a home game in Toronto?
a) Bob Baun   b) Carl Brewer
c) Tim Horton   d) Allan Stanley

   a) Bob Baun completed his playing career with the Leafs after stops in Oakland and Detroit and dressed for Toronto in his last NHL game at Maple Leaf Gardens on October 21, 1972. While Carl Brewer finished his NHL career with a 20-game stint as a Leaf in 1979–80, his final match with the Leafs was at Minnesota on March 25, 1980. Tim Horton's final NHL appearance was at Maple Leaf Gardens but as a Buffalo Sabre on February 20, 1974. Allan Stanley completed his NHL days as a Flyer during the quarterfinals in Philadelphia in April 1969.

5. What was the longest streak of consecutive seasons that a team was out of the playoffs in the Original Six era?
a) 5   b) 6   c) 7   d) 8

   d) 8. The Boston Bruins were out of the playoffs for eight consecutive seasons from 1959–60 to 1966–67. The second-longest streak was Chicago with six seasons from 1946–47 to 1951–52. The Black Hawks missed for five consecutive seasons from 1953–54 to 1957–58 and the New York Rangers missed for five twice—from 1942–43 to 1946–47 and 1950–51 to 1954–55.

6. What is the highest number of players selected as First Team All–Stars from one NHL club?
a) 3   b) 4   c) 5   d) 6

   c) 5. The First All–Star Team for 1963–64 was dominated by five members of the Chicago Black Hawks. Glenn Hall was in goal, Pierre Pilote on defense and Stan Mikita, Kenny Wharram and Bobby Hull on forward. Defenseman Tim Horton was the only non-Hawk to be selected to the team for 1963–64. The 1944–45 Montreal Canadiens also placed five players on the First All–Star Team. Only Detroit's Flash Hollett on defense presented a sweep as Bill Durnan, Butch Bouchard, Elmer Lach, Rocket Richard and Toe Blake were selected.

7. How many times did Bobby Hull win the Art Ross Trophy as the NHL's leading scorer?
a) 2   b) 3   c) 4   d) 5

   b) 3.

		GP	G	A	PTS
1959–60	Bobby Hull, Chicago	70	39	42	81
	Bronco Horvath, Boston	68	39	41	80
1961–62	Bobby Hull, Chicago	70	50	34	84
	Andy Bathgate, New York	70	28	56	84

Bobby Hull awarded Art Ross Trophy with more goals scored than Andy Bathgate

| 1965–66 | Bobby Hull, Chicago | 65 | 54 | 43 | 97 |
| | Stan Mikita, Chicago | 68 | 30 | 48 | 78 |

Jacques Plante stops Bob Pulford in a game in December of 1959, a month after Plante first donned his mask in NHL action.

8. The early 1960s were difficult years for fans of the Boston Bruins. How many times in a row did the Bruins finish in last place?
a) 5   b) 6   c) 7   d) 8

   a) 5. The Boston Bruins finished in sixth place from 1960–61 to 1964–65.

9. The NHL began holding an annual draft in 1963 to allow teams to obtain the rights to amateur players who weren't already considered the property of one of the Original Six teams. Who was the first player chosen in this inaugural Amateur Draft?
a) Ken Dryden   b) Barry Gibbs
c) Peter Mahovlich   d) Garry Monahan

   d) Garry Monahan was chosen first overall by the Montreal Canadiens in the 1963 Amateur Draft and played a total of 14 games with the Habs in 1967–68 and 1968–69 and a further 10 seasons in the NHL with Detroit, Los Angeles, Toronto (on two separate occasions) and Vancouver. Peter Mahovlich was chosen second overall in the 1963 draft by the Detroit Red Wings, with whom he both opened and closed his 16-year NHL career, though he also saw action with the Canadiens and the Pittsburgh Penguins. Ken Dryden was chosen 14th overall by the Boston Bruins in the 1964 draft, but they traded their rights to both Dryden and Alex Campbell to Montreal for Guy Allen and Paul Reid. (Ironically, while Dryden went on to a Hall of Fame career with the Habs, none of the other three saw a single game of NHL action.) Barry Gibbs was chosen first overall by the Bruins in the 1966 draft and went on to a 13-year career with Boston, Minnesota, Atlanta, St. Louis and Los Angeles.

10. Against which team did Terry Sawchuk record his 100th NHL career shutout?
a) Boston   b) Chicago   c) Montreal   d) New York

   b) Chicago. Terry Sawchuk recorded his 100th NHL career shutout as a member of the Toronto Maple Leafs in a 3–0 victory over the Black Hawks on March 4, 1967.

11. Which of the following teams made the fewest playoff appearances during the 25 years of the Original Six era?
a) Boston   b) Chicago   c) New York   d) Toronto

c) New York. Between 1943 and 1967, Montreal made 24 trips to the playoffs, Detroit 22, Toronto 21, Boston 14 and Chicago 12, while the New York Rangers made only seven appearances.

12. The Detroit Red Wings were Stanley Cup finalists in four of the six playoffs between 1961 and 1966. How many individuals played for the Red Wings in all four?
a) 4   b) 5   c) 6   d) 7

b) 5. Alex Delvecchio, Gordie Howe, Bruce MacGregor, Parker MacDonald and Norm Ullman participated in the Stanley Cup finals as members of the Detroit Red Wings in 1961, 1963, 1964 and 1966.

13. How many players were Montreal Canadiens for all five consecutive Stanley Cup championships between 1956 and 1960?
a) 9   b) 10   c) 11   d) 12

d) 12. Jean Beliveau, Don Marshall, Henri Richard, Bernie Geoffrion, Dickie Moore, Maurice Richard, Doug Harvey, Jacques Plante, Jean-Guy Talbot, Tom Johnson, Claude Provost and Bob Turner all played on all five of the Cup-winning Canadiens teams between 1956 and 1960.

14. Name the first Canadien to be the NHL's scoring leader in two consecutive seasons.
a) Jean Beliveau   b) Bernie Geoffrion
c) Elmer Lach   d) Dickie Moore

d) Dickie Moore won the Art Ross Trophy as the NHL's leading scorer in both 1957–58 and 1958–59, marking the first time that a Montreal Canadien had achieved this feat in two consecutive seasons.

15. Name the first player to win three separate awards in one NHL season.
a) Jean Beliveau   b) Gordie Howe
c) Bobby Hull   d) Stan Mikita

d) Stan Mikita of the Chicago Black Hawks was awarded the Art Ross, Hart and Lady Byng awards in 1966–67—and did it again the next year.

16. Who recorded the most penalty minutes in one season in the Original Six era?
a) Lou Fontanato   b) Howie Young
c) John Ferguson   d) Ted Lindsay

b) Howie Young recorded 273 minutes with Detroit in 1962–63. Lou Fontanato recorded 202 minutes with the New York Rangers in 1955–56; Ted Lindsay 184 with Chicago in 1958–59; and John Ferguson 177 with Montreal in 1966–67.

17. Name the only team not to have a Hall of Famer in goal at some time during the 1966–67 season.
a) Boston   b) Detroit   c) Montreal   d) New York

b) Detroit. Roger Crozier, George Gardner and Hank Bassen shared the netminding for the 1966–67 Detroit Red Wings. None of these individuals have been elected to the Hockey Hall of Fame. On the other hand, Boston had Gerry Cheevers and Bernie Parent, Toronto had Johnny Bower and Terry Sawchuk, Chicago had Glenn Hall, Montreal had Gump Worsley and New York had Ed Giacomin in goal in 1966–67.

18. Who was the leading scorer in the 1967 Stanley Cup playoffs?
a) Jean Beliveau   b) Jim Pappin
c) Bob Pulford   d) Peter Stemkowski

b) Jim Pappin.

Playoff Scoring Leaders, 1967

		GP	G	A	PTS
Jim Pappin	Toronto	12	7	8	15
Peter Stemkowski	Toronto	12	5	7	12
Jean Beliveau	Montreal	10	6	5	11
Bob Pulford	Toronto	12	1	10	11

19. Which of the following played their last NHL game as a Leaf?
a) Jacques Plante   b) Dickie Moore
c) Bert Olmstead   d) Billy Reay

c) Bert Olmstead played his last NHL game in the 1962 finals with the Toronto Maple Leafs. Plante and Moore both played for the Leafs, but Plante's last game was with the Boston Bruins and Moore's was with the St. Louis Blues. Billy Reay never played with the Leafs, even though he did coach them in 1957–58 and the beginning of the 1958–59 season.

20. Who was the captain of the Canadiens who won the Cup in 1956?
a) Jean Beliveau   b) Butch Bouchard
c) Doug Harvey   d) Maurice Richard

b) Emile "Butch" Bouchard served as the Canadiens' captain from 1948 to 1956.

Third Period: Expert Trivia

1. Name the captains of each team in 1966–67, the last season of the Original Six.

In 1966–67, George Armstrong captained the Leafs, Jean Beliveau captained the Canadiens, Bob Nevin captained the Rangers, Johnny Bucyk captained the Bruins, Pierre Pilote captained the Black Hawks and Alex Delvecchio captained the Red Wings.

2. Name the five Black Hawks who won the Cup in 1961 who went on to become members of the Hockey Hall of Fame.

Al Arbour, Glenn Hall, Bobby Hull, Stan Mikita and Pierre Pilote all won the Cup as Hawks in 1961 and became Hall of Famers.

3. When was the first Stanley Cup final game played on a Sunday in a Canadian city?

On Sunday, April 24, 1966, Detroit defeated Montreal 3–2 in game one of the Stanley Cup finals at the Montreal Forum.

4. Name the six NHL coaches of the 1966–67 season who are members of the Hockey Hall of Fame. (Hint: Three are honored members as players, the other three as builders.)

Sid Abel, Toe Blake and King Clancy are members of the Hall of Fame as players; Emile Francis, Punch Imlach and Harry Sinden are members as builders. Abel (Detroit), Blake (Montreal), Francis (New York) and Sinden (Boston) coached their teams through the entire 1966–67 season. King Clancy replaced an ailing Imlach for Toronto for 10 games in the middle of the season. Billy Reay—whose Chicago team finished first in 1966–67—is the only NHL coach from that season who has not been inducted.

5. Two Boston Bruins made their only All–Star Game appearance in 1960. Can you name them?

Bob Armstrong and Vic Stasiuk were two of four players chosen to represent Boston in the 1960 All-Star Game. Bob Armstrong was a regular with the Bruins' defense throughout the 1950s and was heading into his last full season with them in 1960–61. Left winger Vic Stasiuk toiled in the NHL from 1949–50 through 1962–63 with Chicago, Detroit, Boston and back to Detroit. He played on three Cup-winning teams with Detroit in the 1950s but never made it to the All–Star Game until 1960, when he represented the Bruins. Armstrong and Stasiuk were winners in their only All–Star Game, though, as the All–Stars defeated the Canadiens 2–1 in the 14th annual game on Saturday, October 1, 1960, in Montreal.

6. **Name the three individuals who made their single appearance on a First All–Star Team in 1964–65.**

Roger Crozier of the Detroit Red Wings was in goal, Norm Ullman of the Detroit Red Wings was at center and Claude Provost of the Montreal Canadiens was on right wing. Ullman was also selected to the NHL's Second All–Star Team in 1966–67.

7. **When was the last time the Stanley Cup finals went to a seventh and deciding game in two consecutive years?**

Toronto defeated Detroit in a seventh and deciding game by a score of 4–0 on April 25, 1964. The following season, Montreal defeated Chicago 4–0 in the seventh game of the finals on May 1, 1965.

8. **Name the six players who led their team in points during 1966–67.**

		Points	*Goals*	*Assists*
Stan Mikita	Chicago	97	35	62
Norm Ullman	Detroit	70	26	44
Bobby Rousseau	Montreal	63	19	44
Phil Goyette	New York	61	12	49
Dave Keon	Toronto	52	19	33
Johnny Bucyk	Boston	48	18	30

9. **Name the two players with more than 500 NHL games who played their last NHL hockey during the 1966–67 season. (Hint: Both of their nicknames are "Red.")**

Leonard "Red" Kelly and Bill "Red" Hay both played their last NHL games during the 1967 playoffs.

10. Why was it sometimes suggested that third-place teams were aiming for fourth in the Original Six era?

All semifinals in the Original Six era matched the third-place team against the first-place team in one series and the fourth-place team against the second-place team in the other. It was often felt that finishing fourth would give a team a better chance, since it put them up against the team that finished second rather than first. The NHL didn't change its first versus third and second versus fourth format until the 1971–72 season.

11. Name the two individuals involved in a one-for-one trade in 1957 that both went on to become members of the Hockey Hall of Fame.

The Boston Bruins traded Terry Sawchuk to the Detroit Red Wings in exchange for Johnny Bucyk and cash on June 10, 1957.

12. There was an unsuccessful attempt to establish a players' association during the 1956–57 season. This first attempt eventually crumbled under tremendous pressure from the ownership of the six NHL franchises. Name the six individuals who were named as the executive of the forerunner of the NHL Players' Association.

Ted Lindsay (Detroit) was named president, Doug Harvey (Montreal) first vice-president, Fernie Flaman (Boston) second vice-president, Gus Mortson (Chicago) third vice-president, Jim Thomson (Toronto) secretary and Bill Gadsby (New York) treasurer.

These pioneers who tried to establish a players' association were labeled troublemakers by the NHL owners. Both Lindsay and Thomson felt their wrath, as both were traded to the then lowly Hawks before the beginning of the next season (1957–58) and Mortson, Gadsby and Harvey were all traded away by their respective teams over the succeeding seasons. Only Fernie Flaman remained on the same team for the remainder of his NHL playing career, last seeing action as a Bruin in 1960–61.

13. Name the five goalies who played for the Toronto Maple Leafs in both the 1965–66 and 1966–67 NHL seasons.

Johnny Bower, Bruce Gamble, Al Smith, Gary Smith and Terry Sawchuk all played for the Leafs in 1965–66 and 1966–67.

14. When was the last time the Leafs finished first overall in the NHL regular season?

The last time the Toronto Maple Leafs led the NHL in points during the regular season was in 1962–63, when only five points separated the first-place Leafs from the fourth-place Red Wings.

NHL, 1962–63

	W	L	T	PTS
Toronto	35	23	12	82
Chicago	32	21	17	81
Montreal	28	19	23	79
Detroit	32	25	13	77
New York	22	36	12	56
Boston	14	39	17	45

15. Name the last goaltender to play the entire regular season for each of the Original Six franchises.

Ed Johnston played for Boston in 1963–64; Glenn Hall played for Chicago in 1961–62; Jacques Plante played for Montreal in 1961–62; Ed Chadwick played for Toronto in 1957–58; Glenn Hall played for Detroit in 1956–57; Lorne "Gump" Worsley played for New York in 1955–56.

16. Name the players who led their team in points for the highest number of seasons in the Original Six era.

Gordie Howe was Detroit's leading point-getter for 14 seasons, Andy Bathgate led New York for eight, Maurice Richard led the Canadiens for four, Frank Mahovlich led Toronto for five, Johnny Bucyk led Boston for four, Stan Mikita led Chicago for four.

17. The Intra-League Draft was established by the NHL during the Original Six era to permit clubs to claim unprotected players from other NHL clubs. The Toronto Maple Leafs acquired four future Hall of Famers through this draft between 1958 and 1964. Can you name them?

The Leafs took Bert Olmstead away from Montreal in the Intra-League Draft of 1958, Al Arbour away from Chicago in 1961, Dickie Moore away from Montreal in 1964 and Terry Sawchuk from Detroit in 1964. The Leafs also lost two future Hall of Famers in the draft during the 1960s. Olmstead was drafted from Toronto by the New York Rangers in 1962 and decided to retire rather than report for 1962–63. Goaltender Gerry Cheevers was drafted away from Toronto by Boston in 1965.

18. When were NHL regular-season games first played in April?

The NHL's regular season extended into April for the first time in the 1965–66 season, with five games on the first weekend of that month.

Saturday, April 2, 1966: Chicago 3 at Montreal 8; and New York 3 at Toronto 3

Sunday, April 3, 1966: Montreal 4 at New York 1; Toronto 3 at Detroit 3; and Chicago 2 at Boston 4

19. Bernie Geoffrion tied the record of 50 goals in a season in 1960–61 and Bobby Hull duplicated this feat the following season. Hull went on to a then record 54 goals in 1965–66. Who was the runner-up in goal-scoring in each of these seasons?

Frank Mahovlich of the Toronto Maple Leafs.

Goal-Scoring Leaders

1960–61	Bernie Geoffrion	Montreal	50
	Frank Mahovlich	Toronto	48
	Dickie Moore	Montreal	35
	Jean Beliveau	Montreal	32
1961–62	Bobby Hull	Chicago	50
	Frank Mahovlich	Toronto	33
	Gordie Howe	Detroit	33
	Claude Provost	Montreal	33
1965–66	Bobby Hull	Chicago	54
	Frank Mahovlich	Toronto	32
	Alex Delvecchio	Detroit	31
	Norm Ullman	Detroit	31

20. Name the three forwards who made up the Uke Line.

Left winger Johnny Bucyk, center Bronco Horvath and right winger Vic Stasiuk made up the Boston Bruins' Uke Line from 1957 to 1961. The line's name recognized the Ukrainian heritage of these three Canadian-born hockey players.

Overtime: Four on Four

1. Name the four players who won the Cup in each of their first five NHL seasons as Montreal Canadiens from 1955–56 to 1959–60.

Claude Provost, Henri Richard, Jean-Guy Talbot and Bob Turner won five consecutive Cups in their first five seasons with the Canadiens. Jean-Guy Talbot had played in three regular-season games with the Canadiens in 1954–55 but joined the club as a regular the following year.

2. Name the only four goalies who participated in the five Stanley Cup final series that the Montreal Canadiens won between 1956 and 1960.

Johnny Bower, Glenn Hall, Jacques Plante and Don Simmons. Plante played for the Canadiens in all 25 games in the five series. Glenn Hall played all five games for the Detroit Red Wings in 1956; Don Simmons played all 11 games for the Boston Bruins in 1957 and 1958; and Johnny Bower played in the Leafs' nine games in 1959 and 1960.

3. Name the four players to be awarded the Norris Trophy during the Original Six era who went on to become head coaches in the NHL.

Red Kelly, Doug Harvey, Tom Johnson and Harry Howell. Pierre Pilote and Jacques Laperriere are the only two Norris winners of the Original Six era who did not hold a head coaching position in the NHL.

Player/Coach	Norris Trophy	Head Coaching
Red Kelly	1954	1967–68 to 1976–77 (Los Angeles, Pittsburgh, Toronto)
Doug Harvey	1955, 1956, 1957, 1958, 1960, 1961, 1962	1961–62 (New York)
Tom Johnson	1959	1970–71 to 1972–73 (Boston)
Harry Howell	1967	1978–79 (Minnesota)

4. Name the four individuals who were members of the 1955 Stanley Cup champion Detroit Red Wings and repeated the feat in 1967 with the Toronto Maple Leafs.

Larry Hillman, Red Kelly, Marcel Pronovost and Terry Sawchuk.

Game 5: Arrival (and a Rival) of Expansion

1967 to 1979

The NHL expanded in a big way for the 1967–68 season after 25 seasons of six teams. Pittsburgh, Philadelphia, St. Louis, Minnesota, Los Angeles and San Francisco/Oakland all added teams to the league, and expansion continued throughout the next decade, with Buffalo and Vancouver being added in 1970, Atlanta and the New York Islanders in 1972 and Washington and Kansas City in 1974. This period also saw the arrival of a competing professional hockey league—the World Hockey Association—which opened with 12 teams for the 1972–73 season. The WHA was the NHL's nemesis throughout its existence, but it didn't last long. At the end of the 1978–79 season, the four surviving franchises were taken in by the older league.

First Period: Who Am I?

1. I was the Boston Bruins goaltender who faced Darryl Sittler on February 7, 1976, when he recorded an all-time record of 10 points in a game.

Dave Reece faced Sittler in this game. His backup was Gerry Cheevers, who had just returned from the WHA. It was Reece's last NHL game.

2. I was the first NHL regular to sign a contract with the WHA.

Bernie Parent of the Toronto Maple Leafs signed with the Miami Screaming Eagles in February 1972. The Eagles never hit the ice, but Parent's contract was honored by the Philadelphia Blazers for the 1972–73 season.

3. I am the only number one pick of the 1970s to play fewer than 500 games in the NHL.

Greg Joly was the number one pick of the Washington Capitals in the 1974 draft and played a total of 365 NHL games with the Caps and the Red Wings between 1974 and 1982.

4. The St. Louis Blues became the first team of the expansion West Division to make the Stanley Cup finals with my overtime goal on May 3, 1968.

When Ron Schock put the puck past Minnesota goalie Cesare Maniago at 2:50 of the second overtime period, he gave St. Louis a 2–1 victory over the North Stars.

5. I played the most games in the WHA without appearing in a single NHL game.

Larry Lund played in 459 regular-season and 59 playoff games, all with the Houston Aeros, between 1972 and 1978.

6. I was claimed in Expansion Drafts by both the Vancouver Canucks in 1970 and the Atlanta Flames in 1972. I went on to a successful NHL career as a general manager and coach.

Pat Quinn played defense with the Toronto Maple Leafs for the 1968–69 and 1969–70 seasons. He was then claimed by Vancouver in the Expansion Draft and played for the Canucks during their first two seasons, 1970–71 and 1971–72. Atlanta claimed Quinn in 1972 and he played with the Flames from 1972–73 until his retirement in 1976–77, serving as the captain in his last two seasons.

7. I was the first selection in the 1967 Expansion Draft.

Goalie Terry Sawchuk was the first player selected (by the Los Angeles Kings from the Toronto Maple Leafs) in the 1967 Expansion Draft.

8. I was the first coach of the Pittsburgh Penguins. (Hint: I had played in the NHL with the Boston Bruins, Chicago Black Hawks and New York Rangers and had a stint as the head coach of the Rangers.)

George "Red" Sullivan was the coach of the Pittsburgh Penguins for their first two NHL seasons, 1967–68 and 1968–69.

9. I was the only person to coach in the expansion West Division for each of its first five seasons (1967–68 to 1971–72).

Red Kelly coached the Los Angeles Kings for their first two seasons, 1967–68 and 1968–69. From there he moved over and coached the Pittsburgh Penguins from 1969–70 until midway through the 1972–73 season.

10. I led the Cleveland Barons in scoring in the only two seasons they were in the NHL.

Dennis Maruk led the Cleveland Barons with 28 goals and 50 assists for 78 points in 1976–77 and again with 36 goals and 35 assists for 71 points in their last season, 1977–78.

11. I was a high-scoring left winger on the Philadelphia Flyers Stanley Cup-winning teams of 1974 and 1975. My best individual season was in 1975–76, when I was named to the First All–Star Team. I went on to become the head coach of the Flyers.

Bill Barber played left wing for the Flyers for 12 seasons, from 1972–73 through 1983–84, recording 420 goals and 463 assists for 883 points in 903 games. Barber was a one-time member of the First All–Star Team and twice made the Second All–Star Team, in 1978–79 and 1980–81. He went on to become the head coach of the Flyers and winner of the Jack Adams Award during the 2000–2001 season.

12. I joined the St. Louis Blues during their first season (1967–68) and emerged as one of the first stars in the NHL's West Division. I hold the NHL record for the most goals scored by an individual player on the visiting team, which I achieved during the 1968–69 season.

Gordon "Red" Berenson saw spot duty with both the Montreal Canadiens and the New York Rangers until he was traded to the St. Louis Blues in November 1967. He established himself as a scoring force in the division, recording a career high 82 points in 76 games in 1968–69. On November 7, 1968, Berenson scored six goals in St. Louis' 8–0 win over the Flyers at Philadelphia.

13. I was Toronto's second choice, the 24th overall, in the 1975 Amateur Draft. I went on to a long and successful career with three NHL clubs and won both the Frank J. Selke Trophy and the Bill Masterton Trophy during my career. But I never saw any NHL game action with the Leafs.

Doug Jarvis was selected by Toronto in the 1975 Draft but traded in June of that year to the Montreal Canadiens for Greg Hubick. Jarvis went on to play 964 consecutive games in the NHL—the longest consecutive streak by any individual player—with Montreal, Washington and Hartford. He was awarded the Frank J. Selke Trophy as the NHL's best defensive forward in 1984 and won the Bill Masterton Trophy in 1987. Meanwhile, Greg Hubick played in 72 games for the Leafs in 1975–76 and a further five games in the NHL as a member of the Vancouver Canucks in 1979–80.

14. I was the first defenseman to win the Conn Smythe Trophy as the most valuable player in the Stanley Cup playoffs.

Serge Savard won the Conn Smythe Trophy as the MVP in the 1969 Stanley Cup playoffs that closed out his second complete season in the NHL. He broke a leg in back-to-back seasons after earning his trophy with the Canadiens but still went on to a successful career, playing on eight Stanley Cup winners with the Canadiens and finishing his playing career with the Winnipeg Jets in 1982–83. He went on to manage the Canadiens and was GM on two Cup-winning teams, in 1986 and 1993. He also faced the Soviet national team as a member of Team Canada '72, Team Canada '76 and the NHL All–Stars in 1979. He is a member of the Hockey Hall of Fame.

15. I was named captain of the Boston Bruins for the 1977–78 season and remained captain until my retirement in 1983.

Wayne Cashman played in 1,027 regular-season and 145 playoff games, all as a Bruin. Dating back from a single game in 1964–65, in the Original Six era, through to his retirement after the 1983 playoffs, Cashman's best individual season was 1973–74, when he finished fourth in NHL scoring with 89 points and was elected as the left winger of the NHL Second All–Star Team.

16. I was the first Red Wing to score 50 goals in an NHL season.

Mickey Redmond scored 52 goals in 1972–73 and again broke the 50-goal barrier with 51 goals in 1973–74. The record for the most goals in a season by a Red Wing had been previously held by Gordie Howe and Frank Mahovlich. Ironically, Redmond was one of three players the Red Wings had received in return for Mahovlich in a January 1971 trade.

17. I hold the record for the most penalty minutes in one NHL season.

Dave "The Hammer" Schultz led the league in penalty minutes for four separate seasons and set an all-time individual NHL record with 472 penalty minutes as a member of the Philadelphia Flyers in 1974–75.

18. In spite of the fact that I scored a then rookie record of 44 goals in my first NHL season, I didn't win the Calder Trophy as the NHL's outstanding rookie.

Rick Martin scored 44 goals and 74 points as a member of the Buffalo Sabres but was runner-up to Ken Dryden, who won the Calder Trophy as rookie of the year in 1971–72. Martin went on to an outstanding career with the Sabres before being traded to L.A. in March 1981. He played his final three games as a member of the Kings in 1981–82.

19. I am the only individual to play for a Stanley Cup winner one season and an Avco Cup winner as WHA champion the following season.

Ted Green was with the 1971–72 Boston Bruins when they were Stanley Cup champions. Then he jumped to the WHA for its first season of operation and was captain of the 1972–73 Avco champions, the New England Whalers.

20. I was the head coach of the last Bruins team to win the Cup.

Tom Johnson coached the 1971–72 Boston Bruins, which was the last time the Bruins won the Cup. Harry Sinden had coached them to their Cup in 1970 but left after a contract dispute and didn't return until he assumed the position of GM for the 1972–73 season. Johnson held the coaching position from 1970–71 until February 1973.

Second Period: Multiple Choice

1. Name the first expansion team to win a playoff game against an Original Six franchise.
a) Philadelphia   b) Minnesota   c) St. Louis   d) Pittsburgh

   b) Minnesota defeated Montreal 6–3 on April 22, 1971. Montreal went on to win that semifinal series four games to two.

2. What was the maximum number of teams in the WHA in one season?
a) 12   b) 13   c) 14   d) 15

   c) 14. The WHA expanded from 12 teams in its first two seasons to 14 teams for 1974–75 and 1975–76 before shrinking back to 12 teams in 1976–77, then eight in 1977–78 and seven in its final season, 1978–79. In both 1974–75 and 1975–76, a franchise relocated—Michigan moved to Baltimore during the 1974–75 season and Denver transferred to Ottawa in the next one—so the WHA had teams in 15 cities in both of these seasons.

3. Name the first season the expansion teams placed more players on the NHL First and Second All–Star teams than the Original Six teams.
a) 1973–74   b) 1974–75   c) 1975–76   d) 1976–77

   c) In 1975–76, the expansion teams placed seven players on All-Star teams while the Original Six teams placed just five. Denis Potvin and Glenn Resch of the Islanders; Bill Barber, Bobby Clarke and Reggie Leach of Philadelphia; and Richard Martin and Gilbert Perreault of Buffalo all placed on the All-Stars in 1975–76. In the previous season, six spots had been taken by expansion and six by Original Six teams.

4. Name the only individual to play with all five Canadiens Cup winners from 1956 to 1960 and also appear in the Stanley Cup finals for the St. Louis Blues for three consecutive years (1968 to 1970).
a) Doug Harvey   b) Dickie Moore
c) Jacques Plante   d) Jean-Guy Talbot

   d) Jean-Guy Talbot. While all four played with Montreal for the five Cup wins from 1956 to 1960, Moore and Harvey only played for St. Louis in the 1968 finals. Plante played in both 1969 and 1970, but Talbot was the only one to appear in all three finals with St. Louis.

5. Which of the following defensemen played their last NHL game as a Montreal Canadien?
a) Bob Turner   b) Dollard St. Laurent
c) Al MacNeil   d) J. C. Tremblay

   d) J. C. Tremblay played his last NHL game as a Montreal Canadien in 1971–72, though he went on to play seven seasons in the WHA. Bob Turner's last NHL game was in 1962–63 with Chicago, Dollard St. Laurent's was in 1962–63 with Chicago and Al MacNeil's was in 1967–68 with Pittsburgh.

6. Phil Esposito played for the Chicago Black Hawks, the Boston Bruins and the New York Rangers during his NHL career. On how many of these teams was Esposito the captain?
a) 0   b) 1   c) 2   d) 3

   b) 1. The only time Phil Esposito was appointed captain was upon his arrival to the New York Rangers in 1975–76 and he reigned there to the beginning of the 1978–79 season. It's a common misconception that Esposito was a captain of the Boston Bruins, but he never wore the "C" on his sweater there. He was one of the assistant captains during his time with the Bruins, however, which lasted from 1967 to 1975. Johnny Bucyk—who had been captain in 1966–67—took over again as team captain in 1973–74 and was still serving when Esposito was traded to the New York Rangers.

7. Pierre Pilote had been the Chicago Black Hawks' captain for seven consecutive seasons when he left at the end of the 1967–68 season. The Hawks would only name a captain for one season, 1969–70, during the seven that followed Pilote's departure (from 1968–69 to 1974–75). Who was this captain?
a) Bobby Hull   b) Pit Martin
c) Stan Mikita   d) Pat Stapleton

   d) Pat Stapleton served as captain during the 1969–70 season—the only time from 1968–69 to 1974–75 that Chicago appointed a captain. Mikita and Martin shared the captaincy in 1975–76 and 1976–77 and, oddly enough, Bobby Hull never served as the captain of the Black Hawks.

8. During the 1970s, Darryl Sittler, Bob Gainey and Ray Bourque were all chosen at the same position in the Entry Draft. In which overall position were they selected in the

NHL draft in their respective years?
a) second   b) fourth   c) sixth   d) eighth

d) Sittler was chosen from the London Knights by the Toronto Maple Leafs in the 1970 Amateur Draft. Gainey was chosen from the Peterborough Petes by the Montreal Canadiens in 1973. Ray Bourque was chosen from the Verdon Eperviers by the Boston Bruins in 1979. All were the eighth overall pick.

9. Certainly one of the failures of NHL expansion was the hapless Oakland Seals/California Golden Seals/Cleveland Barons. How many times in the 11 seasons of this NHL franchise (from 1967–68 to the end of the 1977–78 season, when the team was folded and merged with the Minnesota North Stars) did the team make the Stanley Cup playoffs?
a) 1   b) 2   c) 3   d) 4

b) 2. The franchise's only two appearances in the playoffs were as the Oakland Seals in their second and third seasons of operation. In the 1969 Stanley Cup playoffs, Los Angeles defeated Oakland in four games to three in the quarterfinals, and that was the only time that this franchise would even win a playoff game. In 1970, the Pittsburgh Penguins swept the Seals in four straight games in the quarterfinals.

10. How many teams have retired the number 4 to honor a player? (Hint: All players honored with retiring the number 4 played their last NHL game during the 1970s.)
a) 2   b) 3   c) 4   d) 5

b) 3. Number 4 has been retired by the Boston Bruins to honor Bobby Orr, by the Canadiens to honor Jean Beliveau and by Philadelphia to honor Barry Ashbee. Orr last played for the Bruins during the 1975–76 season, although he saw action in part of two seasons as a member of the Chicago Black Hawks. He retired early in the 1978–79 season and the Black Hawks didn't hang up Orr's number 4. Jean Beliveau retired from the Canadiens after the end of the 1971 playoffs. Barry Ashbee saw his last NHL action during the 1974 semifinal series with the Flyers, when he suffered a career-ending eye injury. Tragically, Ashbee died of leukemia three years later.

11. How many individuals who played in the World Hockey Association were still actively playing in the NHL at the end of the 2000–2001 season?

a) 0   b) 1   c) 2   d) 3

   b) 1. Mark Messier is the only player who had played in the WHA who was still playing in the NHL at the end of the 2000–2001 season.

12. In how many consecutive seasons did Phil Esposito win the Art Ross Trophy as the scoring leader?
a) 4   b) 5   c) 6   d) 7

   a) 4. Phil Esposito was the leading scorer for the four consecutive seasons between 1970–71 and 1973–74. Bobby Orr won the Art Ross as the scoring leader in 1969–70 and 1974–75, at both ends of Phil Esposito's consecutive scoring championships. Esposito was the scoring leader on one other occasion, in 1968–69.

13. Leafs captain Dave Keon left the NHL after the 1974–75 season and played the following four in the WHA. Which of the following teams signed Keon to his first WHA contract?
a) The New England Whalers   b) The Indianapolis Racers
c) The Minnesota Fighting Saints   d) The Denver Spurs

   c) The Minnesota Fighting Saints. It was clear to Keon after the 1974–75 season that the Maple Leafs under Harold Ballard no longer wished to retain his services, despite an outstanding 15-year, Hall of Fame career with the club. The Toronto Toros of the WHA owned Keon's player rights but traded them to Minnesota, with whom Keon signed as a free agent. The Minnesota Fighting Saints folded in February 1976 and Keon then signed with Indianapolis for the rest of the season. He opened 1976–77 as a member of the new Minnesota Fighting Saints franchise and was traded to New England via Edmonton in January 1977. He finished his WHA career with the Whalers in 1978–79 and stayed on with them as they became the Hartford Whalers of the NHL until the end of the 1981–82 season, when he retired from professional hockey.

14. Which of the following was a head coach for all seven seasons of the WHA?
a) Jacques Demers   b) Bill Dineen
c) Harry Neale   d) Glen Sonmor

   b) Bill Dineen was a veteran of five NHL seasons between 1953–54 and 1957–58 with the Detroit Red Wings and Chicago Black Hawks and continued to play minor professional hockey until the end of the 1970–71 season. He was a head coach for all seven seasons that the WHA

Bobby Orr celebrates his overtime goal that gave the 1970 Boston Bruins their first Stanley Cup in twenty-nine years.

operated, leading his teams into the playoffs on every occasion and twice winning league championships. He was head coach of the Houston Aeros for the first six years of the WHA and after the franchise folded spent his last season in the league as the head coach of the New England Whalers. He returned to a head coaching position with the Philadelphia Flyers, taking over from Paul Holmgren during the 1991–92 season, and coached there until the end of the next season.

15. Which of the following cities was not represented by a WHA franchise in a first player draft held in February 1972?
a) Calgary   b) Cleveland   c) Dayton   d) Miami

b) Cleveland. While Cleveland iced the Crusaders in the WHA's first season, 1972–73, a team representing the city hadn't been at the table for the WHA draft of 1972. The Calgary Broncos, Dayton Arrows and Miami Screaming Eagles all took part in the WHA's first player draft in 1972. The Dayton franchise was transferred to Houston, Texas, in March 1972 and became known as the Houston Aeros. The Miami Screaming Eagles, who had made news in February by signing goalie Bernie Parent of the Toronto Maple Leafs, were transferred to Philadelphia as the Blazers in June 1972. The Calgary Broncos had been dropped from the league in April 1972 and the franchise was replaced by the Cleveland Crusaders in June.

16. Name the first NHL season in which there were two 50-goal scorers.
a) 1968–69   b) 1969–70   c) 1970–71   d) 1971–72

c) 1970–71. The first time the NHL had two 50-goal scorers in the same season, both Phil Esposito and Johnny Bucyk of the Boston Bruins achieved this feat. Phil Esposito ended the season with an amazing 76 goals in 78 games and Johnny Bucyk reached 51 goals as a 35-year-old in his 16th NHL season. Bucyk remains the oldest person to achieve the milestone of 50 goals in one NHL season. In the following season, three individuals—Phil Esposito, Vic Hadfield and Bobby Hull—all reached the 50-goal plateau.

17. In which season did the NHL adopt the standard practice of home teams wearing white and visiting teams wearing colored uniforms?
a) 1951–52   b) 1954–55   c) 1970–71   d) 1974–75

Both a) 1951–52 and c) 1970–71. The 1951–52 NHL teams agreed to wear basic white uniforms at home and colored uniforms on the road. This was reversed for 1954–55, and that remained the norm until 1969–70. In 1970–71, the NHL went back to home teams wearing white and visiting teams wearing colors, which is the standard practice to this day.

18. Which of the following players won an individual NHL award as a member of the California/Oakland Seals?
a) Ted Hampson   b) Reggie Leach
c) Craig Patrick   d) Charlie Simmer

a) Ted Hampson won the Bill Masterton Trophy as a member of the Oakland Seals in 1968–69. While the other players named have all won individual NHL awards (Reggie Leach won the Conn Smythe, Craig Patrick won the Lester Patrick and Charlie Simmer won the Bill Masterton), none of them earned these awards during their years with the Seals franchise.

19. Which of the following defensemen played their last NHL game as a Chicago Black Hawk?
a) Pierre Pilote   b) Elmer Vasko
c) Pat Stapleton   d) Wayne Hillman

c) Pat Stapleton. Pilote's last NHL game was as a Maple Leaf in 1968–69, Vasko's was as a member of the Minnesota North Stars in 1969–70 and Hillman's was as a member of the Philadelphia Flyers in 1972–73. Stapleton's last NHL game was in 1972–73 with the Chicago Black Hawks—even though he played several seasons in the WHA.

20. Which of the following was the first player to score 50 goals in a season on one of the NHL's expansion teams?
a) Bill Barber   b) Bobby Clarke
c) Rick MacLeish   d) Gilbert Perreault

c) Rick MacLeish of the Philadelphia Flyers recorded 50 goals in the 1972–73 season, becoming the first player from any of the expansion teams to accomplish this feat.

Third Period: Expert Trivia

1. The NHL doubled from six to 12 teams in 1967. Name the three new teams from cities that had already been in the league.

The Pittsburgh Pirates played in the NHL from 1925–26 to 1929–30; the Philadelphia Quakers (the relocated Pittsburgh franchise) played in 1930–31; and the St. Louis Eagles (the relocated Ottawa Senators) played in 1934–35.

2. The Kansas City Scouts and the Washington Capitals were NHL expansion franchises in 1974–75. Where is the Kansas City franchise now located?

Kansas City relocated to Colorado as the Rockies in 1976–77 and then to New Jersey as the Devils in 1982–83.

3. Name the first expansion team to win a playoff series over an Original Six franchise.

The Philadelphia Flyers defeated the New York Rangers in the 1974 semifinals by four games to three. The Flyers then went on to defeat the Boston Bruins four games to two to win their first Stanley Cup.

4. Name the first player from each of the 1967–68 expansion teams to make the NHL First All–Star Team.

Glenn Hall of the St. Louis Blues (1968–69); Bernie Parent of the Philadelphia Flyers (1973–74); Marcel Dionne of the Los Angeles Kings (1976–77); and Randy Carlyle of the Pittsburgh Penguins (1980–81). The Oakland Seals/California Golden Seals/Cleveland Barons didn't place a player on the First All–Star Team and the Minnesota North Stars/Dallas Stars have yet to place one.

5. The Oakland Seals/California Golden Seals/Cleveland Barons never won a playoff series. Which of the other five 1967–68 expansion teams was the last to finally win a playoff series?

Philadelphia was the last of the five to win a playoff series. The St. Louis Blues and the Minnesota North Stars both won series in the 1968 playoffs. The Los Angeles Kings won a quarterfinal round in 1969 and the Pittsburgh Penguins won a quarterfinal series in 1970. The Flyers lost out on their first three attempts but finally won a quarterfinal round in Minnesota in 1973.

6. Name the first captain of each of the 1967–68 expansion teams.

Bob Baun (the Oakland Seals/California Seals), Bob Woytowich (the Minnesota North Stars), Bob Wall (the Los Angeles Kings), Lou Angotti (the Philadelphia Flyers), Ab McDonald (the Pittsburgh Penguins) and Al Arbour (the St. Louis Blues).

7. Brothers Barclay, Bill and Bob Plager at times made up half of the St. Louis defense. Which of them played his entire NHL career with the Blues and which played the most games as a Blue?

Barclay Plager played all of his 614 regular-season and 68 playoff games with the St. Louis Blues. Bob Plager played his first 29 games with the New York Rangers and then 615 regular-season and 74 playoff games with the Blues. Bill began and ended his career as a member of the Minnesota North Stars, played one season in Atlanta, 1972–73, and played 127 regular-season and 19 playoff games as a Blue between 1968 and 1972.

8. Name the two players who took part in all seven WHA seasons but never played in the NHL.

Don Burgess took part in 446 regular-season games over the seven WHA seasons, playing in Philadelphia, Vancouver, San Diego and Indianapolis. Pierre Guite played in 376 regular-season WHA games in Quebec, Baltimore, Cincinnati and Edmonton.

9. The Avco Cup was awarded to the winner of the WHA playoff series. Which WHA team won the most Avco awards?

The Winnipeg Jets were WHA playoff champions on three occasions: in 1976, when they defeated the Houston Aeros four games to one; in 1978, when they defeated the New England Whalers in four straight; and in 1979, the WHA's final year, when they defeated Edmonton four games to two.

10. Name the only WHA playoff championship team that didn't eventually become an NHL franchise.

The Houston Aeros won the Avco Cup as WHA champions in both 1974 and 1975, but the Aeros suspended operations in July 1978, a full year before a merger was agreed to between the WHA and NHL teams. Houston is still waiting for its first taste of NHL hockey.

11. Name the only three goalies to play in the net for the Cleveland Barons in the NHL.

Gilles Meloche, Gary Edwards and Gary Simmons. All three goalies played for the Cleveland Barons during the 1976–77 season and Meloche and Edwards tended the nets in 1977–78.

12. While widely recognized as an outstanding general manager and coach, Glen Sather spent his first 10 years in the NHL as a journeyman left winger. Name the six different NHL teams he played with during his 658 regular-season and 72 playoff games from 1966 to 1976.

Glen Sather played for Boston, Pittsburgh, the New York Rangers, St. Louis, Montreal and Minnesota. He played five games with the Bruins in 1966–67 and went on to play complete seasons with them through to the 1968–69 season. In 1969–70, and midway through 1970–71, he played with the Penguins. He played with the Rangers from 1970–71 through to the 1973–74 season, when he was traded to the Blues. He finished that season with the Blues and played with the Montreal Canadiens in 1974–75. He played his final NHL season as a member of the Minnesota North Stars in 1975–76.

13. Name the two head coaches of the New York Islanders during their first NHL season, 1972–73. (Hint: They were both former New York Rangers centers.)

Phil Goyette and Earl Ingarfield. Goyette coached the Islanders to a 6–38–4 start in the 1972–73 season before he was replaced by Earl Ingarfield, who recorded 6–22–2 for the rest of the season. Goyette and Ingarfield had been teammates as Rangers centers from 1963 to 1967, but this was the only time either coached in the NHL.

14. Name the two members of the Hockey Hall of Fame who both played their final NHL game in December 1969 as a member of the Toronto Maple Leafs.

Johnny Bower and Marcel Pronovost. Bower had retired at the conclusion of the 1969 Stanley Cup playoffs but returned to play one game in goal for the Leafs on December 10, 1969, in a 6–3 loss to the Canadiens at the Montreal Forum. A month before this game, he had turned 45, but he played a solid game in the net, stopping 33 of 38 before the Canadiens scored an empty-net goal with six seconds to go. Marcel Pronovost played his final game as a member of the Leafs on December 27, 1969, in a 4–1 win over the visiting St. Louis Blues but continued to play in the Central Hockey League as player-coach with the Tulsa Oilers during 1969–70 and into the 1970–71 season.

15. Who won the Gordie Howe Trophy as the most valuable player in the WHA in its final season of operation, 1978–79?

Goaltender Dave Dryden of the Edmonton Oilers was voted the most valuable player, in addition to winning the Ben Hatskin Trophy as the best goaltender for the league's final season of operation, 1978–79.

16. Name the two versatile NHL veterans (they played both defense and forward) who were the first captains of NHL expansion teams during the 1970s.

Doug Mohns and Ed Westfall. Doug Mohns was the first captain of the Washington Capitals in 1974–75. Mohns was a 22-year NHL veteran and played for Boston, Chicago, Minnesota, Atlanta and Washington. Mohns retired after the 1974–75 season. Ed Westfall was an 18-year veteran who'd spent his first 11 seasons with the Boston Bruins, where he played on the Cup-winning teams of 1969–70 and 1971–72. He was claimed by the New York Islanders in 1972 and named their first captain, a position he held into the 1976–77 season. He retired from the Islanders following the 1978–79 season—the year before their first Stanley Cup victory.

17. The NHL was divided into East and West divisions for seven seasons from 1967–68 to 1973–74. On only one occasion during those seven seasons did two teams from the same division meet in the Stanley Cup finals. In what year did this happen?

The Boston Bruins finished first in the East Division in 1971–72, then defeated the second-place New York Rangers four games to two in the Stanley Cup finals. For the first three seasons after expansion (1967–68 to 1969–70), the Stanley Cup finals had been arranged as the winner of the East against the winner of the West. This format was changed for the next four seasons, to allow crossover playoffs between East and West in the semifinals to ensure the two best teams met in the finals. However, on only this one occasion—in 1972—did the two teams from one division play off for the Cup.

Stanley Cup Finalists

	East Division	West Division
1967–68	Montreal*	St. Louis
1968–69	Montreal*	St. Louis
1969–70	Boston*	St. Louis
1970–71	Montreal*	Chicago
1972–73	Montreal*	Chicago
1973–74	Boston	Philadelphia*

*Stanley Cup winner

18. Who established a league record by playing in his 631st consecutive NHL game during the 1975–76 season?

Garry Unger's consecutive-game streak began on February 24, 1968, in his rookie season with the Toronto Maple Leafs. He was involved in a blockbuster trade that included sending Frank Mahovlich to the Detroit Red Wings on March 3, 1968. Unger was later traded to the St. Louis Blues and was playing there when he broke the consecutive-game record. He went on to play for a then record 914 consecutive games until December 21, 1979, as a member of the Atlanta Flames, which still ranks second as the all-time record for the most consecutive NHL games.

19. Who scored the most goals in the first season of the WHA, 1972–73?

Danny Lawson had a 219-game career in the NHL before joining the WHA. He'd recorded 28 goals and 29 assists for 57 points in these games and not a single goal in his playoff appearances. However, he scored 61 goals and 45 assists for 106 points in 78 games for the Philadelphia Blazers in the first season of the WHA, 1972–73.

1972–73 Goal-scoring in the WHA

Danny Lawson	Philadelphia	61
Tom Webster	New England	53
Bobby Hull	Winnipeg	51
Ron Ward	New York	51
Andre Lacroix	Philadelphia	50

20. Name the only player ever to be chosen first overall in the NHL Entry Draft by the Philadelphia Flyers.

Mel Bridgman was the Flyers' first choice overall in the 1975 Entry Draft. The two-time Cup champions managed to obtain the first pick by sending Bill Clement and Don McLean and a draft pick to the Washington Capitals, who owned the first pick. Bridgman made the Flyers as a rookie in 1975–76 and played for more than six seasons with them. He also played for Calgary, New Jersey, Detroit and Vancouver in an NHL career that ended in Vancouver, where he spent his final season in 1988–89.

Overtime: Four on Four

1. Name the four clubs from the expansion West Division who qualified for the Stanley Cup playoffs in 1967–68.

The first-place Philadelphia Flyers, the second-place Los Angeles Kings, the third-place St. Louis Blues and the fourth-place Minnesota North Stars. All the West Division playoffs went to a maximum seven games that year. St. Louis upset Philadelphia four games to three and Minnesota did the same to Los Angeles. St. Louis then eliminated Minnesota in seven games to advance to the Stanley Cup finals against the Montreal Canadiens.

2. **Derek Sanderson had an outstanding first five seasons with the Boston Bruins. He won the Calder Trophy as the NHL's outstanding rookie in 1967–68 and played on Stanley Cup-winning teams in 1970 and 1972. After receiving a reported $1,000,000 for playing eight games for the WHA in 1972–73, he returned to the Bruins for parts of the 1972–73 and 1973–74 NHL seasons. He was clearly not the same player, however, as he moved on through four NHL teams between 1974–75 and 1977–78, when he played his last NHL hockey. Name the four teams he played with after the Bruins.**

The New York Rangers, the St. Louis Blues, the Vancouver Canucks and the Pittsburgh Penguins. The Bruins traded Sanderson to the Rangers prior to the 1974–75 season. He was then traded to the St. Louis Blues early in 1975–76. He was traded to Vancouver during the 1976–77 season and signed as a free agent with the Pittsburgh Penguins, where he saw his last NHL action, during 1977–78.

3. **The Bill Masterton Memorial Trophy is awarded to the player who exhibits perseverance, sportsmanship and dedication to hockey. Name the first four winners of this award.**

Bill Masterton Trophy Winners: Claude Provost (Montreal Canadiens) 1968; Ted Hampson (Oakland Seals) 1969; Pit Martin (Chicago Black Hawks) 1970; and Jean Ratelle (New York Rangers) 1971.

4. **Name the only four captains of the Atlanta Flames.**

Keith McCreary (1972–73 to 1974–75); Pat Quinn (1975–76 to 1976–77); Tom Lysiak (1977–78 to 1978–79); and Jean Pronovost (1979–80).

Game 6: The Wayne and Mario Show

1979 to 1993

Hockey fans were treated to repeated examples of the outstanding skills of Wayne Gretzky and, later, Mario Lemieux during these years. But they were exciting for more than that very good reason. The WHA ceased to exist after the 1978–79 season, which meant that all the best professional players were back in one league. The New York Islanders won four straight Stanley Cup championships before the Edmonton Oilers took over as the most recent NHL dynasty. The NHL began to expand again as it headed into the 1990s, adding the San Jose Sharks in 1991–92 and teams in Ottawa and Tampa Bay for 1992–93.

First Period: Who Am I?

1. I was traded by Toronto to the Colorado Rockies with Lanny McDonald for Pat Hickey and Wilf Paiement in December 1979. I went on to coach after a 13-year NHL playing career.

Joel Quenneville also hit the ice with New Jersey, Hartford and Washington. After finishing his NHL playing career—and starting another in the American Hockey League—he returned to the NHL as an assistant coach with the Quebec Nordiques/Colorado Avalanche from 1994 to 1997.

He was named head coach of the St. Louis Blues midway through the 1996–97 season and won the Jack Adams Award as coach of the year in St. Louis in 1999–2000.

2. I was the first captain of the San Jose Sharks. (Hint: I was a Norris Trophy winner.)

Doug Wilson spent most of his career with Chicago and won the Norris Trophy as the NHL's outstanding defenseman. He was traded to San Jose prior to their first season, 1991–92, and served as their captain for their first two.

3. I coached the Hartford Whalers for three different stretches during the 1980s. (Hint: I was the general manager of a different franchise at the end of the 2000–2001 season.)

Larry Pleau's first stretch as the Hartford Whalers' head coach began on February 20, 1981, and continued through to the end of the 1981–82 season. Pleau had also become general manager for 1981–82, and at the beginning of the 1982–83 season, he named Larry Kish as head coach. Pleau fired Kish and put himself behind the bench on January 15, 1983, and coached until an illness forced John Cunniff to replace him for the last eight games of the season. Emile Francis replaced Pleau as general manager and Jack Evans was named coach for the 1983–84 season, but Pleau stayed with the Whalers organization and had his third stretch as head coach when he replaced Evans on February 7, 1988. Pleau coached the Whalers through the rest of that year and the entire 1988–89 season. He was replaced by Rick Ley for 1989–90. Pleau coached in a total of 224 regular-season games over five seasons with the Whalers and also in 10 playoff games in the 1988 and 1989 Stanley Cup playoffs. Larry Pleau has been the general manager of the St. Louis Blues for the last four NHL seasons.

4. I am the only coach to lead the Calgary Flames to a Stanley Cup victory.

Terry Crisp's Calgary Flames defeated the Montreal Canadiens four games to two in the 1989 Stanley Cup finals. Bob Johnson had led the Flames into the finals three years earlier but was defeated by Montreal four games to one in the 1986 finals.

5. I succeeded Bobby Clarke as captain of the Philadelphia Flyers.

Dave Poulin became captain of the Flyers in his second full season, 1984–85, after Bobby Clarke's retirement. He was captain to the midway point of the 1989–90 season, at which time he was traded to the Boston Bruins.

6. I was the leading scorer for the Pittsburgh Penguins in the 1992 Stanley Cup finals. (Hint: I represented Canada in both the 1987 and 1991 Canada Cup tournaments.)

Rick Tocchet played his entire NHL career with the Philadelphia Flyers until he was traded to Pittsburgh in February 1992—just in time to take part in the Penguins' second Stanley Cup victory. He recorded a series-leading two goals and six assists for eight points in the four-game victory over the Chicago Blackhawks. Tocchet went on to play for Los Angeles, Boston, Washington, Phoenix before returning to Philadelphia.

7. I led three different Canadian franchises in team scoring in three consecutive seasons.

Vincent Damphousse led the Toronto Maple Leafs in scoring in the 1990–91 season with 73 points, the Edmonton Oilers in 1991–92 with 89 and the Montreal Canadiens in 1992–93 with 97.

8. I hold the record for the most points by a rookie defenseman in one season and I've played in six NHL cities and on four Cup winners during my NHL career.

Larry Murphy has moved into second place behind Gordie Howe in all-time NHL games played. He was drafted fourth overall in 1980 by the Los Angeles Kings and recorded 76 points in the 1980–81 season—a record that still stands. He has gone on to play for Washington, Minnesota, Pittsburgh, Toronto and Detroit. He was on four Cup winners, two in Pittsburgh and two in Detroit.

9. I was the first player who wasn't a member of the French Connection of Gilbert Perreault, Rick Martin and Rene Robert to lead the Buffalo Sabres in scoring.

Danny Gare led the team in scoring with 85 points in the 1980–81 season, the Sabres' 11th. In the first 10, the team scoring had been dominated by Perreault seven times, Martin twice and Robert once.

10. I was the captain of the United States team that captured the gold medal at the 1980 Winter Olympics.

Mike Eruzione scored the winning goal against the Soviets that made the Miracle on Ice possible. He retired following the 1980 Olympic Games.

11. I was the first defenseman to record 1,000 points in NHL regular-season action.

Denis Potvin recorded his 1,000th NHL point on April 4, 1987, and retired at the end of the 1987–88 season with a total of 1,052 points in 1,060 regular-season NHL games. Potvin won the Norris Trophy as the NHL's outstanding defenseman on three occasions, was selected to the NHL's First All–Star Team five times and was the captain of the New York Islanders in all four of their Stanley Cup victories. He was inducted into the Hockey Hall of Fame in 1990.

12. I was selected second overall in the 1984 Entry Draft behind Mario Lemieux.

Kirk Muller was the second choice overall (by the New Jersey Devils) in the 1984 Entry Draft. Muller spent seven seasons with New Jersey before being traded to Montreal prior to the 1991–92 NHL season and was an integral part of the 1993 Stanley Cup champion team. He briefly served as the Canadiens' captain during the strike-shortened 1994–95 season, before being traded to the New York Islanders. Since then, he's done stints in Toronto and Florida and closed the 2000–2001 season with the Dallas Stars.

13. I hold the record for the most goals scored by a player on a first-year NHL team.

Blaine Stoughton recorded 56 goals for the 1979–80 Hartford Whalers, one of the four ex-WHA teams to join the NHL for that season. Stoughton had played three seasons in the NHL with Pittsburgh and Toronto before moving to the WHA, where he recorded 52 goals with the Cincinnati Stingers in 1976–77. Later, he played for Indianapolis and New England/Hartford and moved back to the NHL with the Whalers.

14. I was drafted 210th overall in the 1975 Entry Draft but went on to an outstanding 17-year NHL career, recording 1,069 points in 1,111 regular-season games with the team that drafted me. And I've served as general manager of this same NHL franchise since 1997.

Dave Taylor. The Los Angeles Kings used their final pick in the 1975 Entry Draft (210th) to select him, but Taylor ended up playing in more regular-season NHL games (1,111) and recording more points (1,069) than any other player selected. Taylor's most productive NHL seasons came as a member of the Triple Crown Line with Marcel Dionne and Charlie Simmer. Taylor finished his playing career with the Kings in the 1993–94 season and has been their general manager since 1997.

15. I was the only player to wear number 77 for the Edmonton Oilers.

Garry Unger played for the Edmonton Oilers for portions of three seasons, from 1980–81 to 1982–83, and was the only player who wore number 77.

16. I hold the record for the most goals and points in the playoffs in my rookie season.

Dino Ciccarelli of the Minnesota North Stars recorded a rookie record of 14 goals and 21 points in 19 playoff games in 1981.

17. I sported number 99 for Toronto while the "other number 99" was starting out his Hall of Fame career in Edmonton.

Wilf Paiement wore number 99 for the Leafs from his arrival in December 1979 until he was traded to Quebec in March 1982.

18. I am the only individual to take part in the Stanley Cup playoffs in every one of my 20 NHL seasons.

Larry Robinson participated in 20 consecutive playoffs, from 1973 through 1992. Robinson was a Montreal Canadien for his first 17 seasons and spent his last three with the Los Angeles Kings.

19. I am the first goaltender to record 16 wins in a single NHL playoff season.

Grant Fuhr of the Edmonton Oilers recorded 16 wins in the 1988 Stanley Cup playoffs.

20. I am the only player to score three shorthanded goals in one game.

Theoren Fleury recorded three shorthanded goals in an 8–4 Calgary victory that was played in St. Louis on March 9, 1991.

Second Period: Multiple Choice

1. Who was in goal for the Edmonton Oilers when they won the Stanley Cup in 1990?
a) Andy Moog   b) Grant Fuhr
c) Bill Ranford   d) Bob Essensa

   c) Bill Ranford not only played goal for Edmonton during the final game but was awarded the Conn Smythe Trophy as the most valuable player in the 1990 playoffs.

2. How many consecutive Art Ross awards did Wayne Gretzky win?
a) 6   b) 7   c) 8   d) 9

   b) 7. Wayne Gretzky won the Art Ross Trophy as the top NHL scorer for a record seven consecutive seasons, from 1980–81 to 1986–87. Marcel Dionne edged Gretzky out in 1979–80 and Mario Lemieux was the leading scorer in 1987–88.

3. Name the first NHL season in which there were no players left from the Original Six era, which ended in 1966–67?
a) 1981–82   b) 1982–83   c) 1983–84   d) 1984–85

   c) 1983–84. The last three "survivors" from the Original Six era were Wayne Cashman, Serge Savard and Carol Vadnais, all of whom finished their NHL careers in 1982–83.

4. Which of the following did not have a brother who played in the NHL?
a) Ray Bourque   b) Wayne Gretzky
c) Mario Lemieux   d) Mark Messier

   a) Ray Bourque. Wayne Gretzky's brother Brent played 13 games in the NHL with the Tampa Bay Lightning in 1993–94 and 1994–95. Mario Lemieux's brother Alain played a total of 119 regular-season and 19 playoff games with St. Louis, Quebec and Pittsburgh between 1981–82 and 1986–87. And Mark Messier's brother Paul played nine games for the Colorado Rockies in 1978–79.

5. The following four teams were accepted from the WHA as NHL expansion franchises in 1979. Which never won an Avco Cup as the WHA champion?
a) The Edmonton Oilers   b) The New England/Hartford Whalers   c) The Quebec Nordiques   d) The Winnipeg Jets

a) The Edmonton Oilers never did win an Avco, but they managed to capture the first five Stanley Cup championships awarded to any of these franchises. The Quebec Nordiques/Colorado Avalanche won their first Stanley Cup in 1996. The New England/Hartford Whalers/Carolina Hurricanes and Winnipeg Jets/Phoenix Coyotes are still waiting for their first Stanley Cup championship.

Avco Cup Champions

New England Whalers	1973
Houston Aeros	1974, 1975
Winnipeg Jets	1976, 1978, 1979
Quebec Nordiques	1977

6. The following players were all selected in the 1987 Entry Draft. Who was the last to be selected by an NHL team?
a) Eric Desjardins   b) John LeClair
c) Joe Sakic   d) Brendan Shanahan

a) Eric Desjardins was the 38th player selected (by the Montreal Canadiens) in the 1987 Entry Draft. John LeClair was 33rd, also selected by the Montreal Canadiens. Joe Sakic was the 15th pick, chosen by the Quebec Nordiques. Brendan Shanahan was chosen second overall, by the New Jersey Devils.

7. How many of the four teams that survived the WHA to become expansion franchises made the 1980 Stanley Cup playoffs in their first season in the NHL?
a) 0   b) 1   c) 2   d) 3

c) 2. Both the Hartford Whalers and the Edmonton Oilers made the Stanley Cup playoffs in their first season in the NHL, while Quebec and Winnipeg missed the playoffs. Montreal swept Hartford in a best-of-five series and Philadelphia swept Edmonton.

8. Which of the following franchises was the last to win a playoff series in the NHL?

a) The Edmonton Oilers   b) The Hartford Whalers
c) The Quebec Nordiques   d) The Winnipeg Jets

b) Hartford couldn't win a playoff series until 1986, their seventh year in the NHL, when they swept the Quebec Nordiques in the division semifinals. They went on to lose in overtime in the seventh game of the division finals to the Montreal Canadiens. The Winnipeg Jets hadn't won a playoff series until the division semifinals in 1985, when they defeated Calgary three games to one but were swept by Edmonton in the division finals in four games. Quebec won its first playoff series in 1982 when they defeated Montreal 3–2 in the fifth and deciding game to take the division semifinals. Quebec then defeated Boston in the division finals but was eliminated by the Islanders in four straight in the conference finals. The Oilers won their first playoff round in 1981 when they swept the Montreal Canadiens in three straight in the preliminary round and then were defeated by the Islanders in six games in the quarterfinals.

9. How many times did Wayne Gretzky lead the NHL in goals scored?
a) 5   b) 6   c) 7   d) 8

a) 5. Gretzky led the NHL in scoring on five different occasions as an Edmonton Oiler, scoring 92 in 1981–82, 71 in 1982–83, 87 in 1983–84, 73 in 1984–85 and 62 in 1986–87.

10. What is the largest number of Canadian cities to have teams in the NHL in a single season?
a) 6   b) 7   c) 8   d) 9

c) 8. When the Ottawa Senators joined the NHL for the 1992–93 season, it brought the complement of Canadian cities represented in the league to eight and there were eight Canadian teams in the NHL for three seasons, from 1992–93 to 1994–95.

11. Who was the captain of the Ottawa Senators for their first season, 1992–93?
a) Laurie Boschman   b) Mark Lamb
c) Brad Marsh   d) Brad Shaw

a) Laurie Boschman served as the Senator's captain for his final NHL season, 1992–93. Brad Shaw and Mark Lamb shared Ottawa's captaincy with Gord Dineen in 1993–94.

12. The Expansion Draft of 1979 allowed the surviving WHA franchises that were joining the league to select unprotected players from the existing NHL clubs. Who was the first player selected in the 1979 draft?
a) Cam Connor   b) Dave Farrish
c) Al Hangsleben   d) Peter Marsh

   d) Peter Marsh was selected first, by Winnipeg from Montreal. Cam Connor was claimed next, from Montreal by Edmonton, followed by Al Hangsleben, from Montreal by Hartford, and Dave Farrish, from the New York Rangers by Quebec.

13. When was sudden-death overtime reintroduced for regular-season games?
a) 1979–80   b) 1981–82   c) 1983–84   d) 1985–86

   c) 1983–84. The NHL reintroduced a five-minute sudden-death overtime period at the end of tied regular-season games for the 1983–84 season. (Overtime hadn't been played after regular-season games since 1942.)

14. For how many years did the NHL's first Atlanta franchise play out of that city?
a) 6   b) 7   c) 8   d) 9

   c) 8. The Atlanta Flames were an expansion franchise for the 1972–73 season and played out of Georgia through to the end of the 1979–80 season, when they relocated to Calgary. Atlanta iced competitive teams throughout their eight years in the city, qualifying for the Stanley Cup playoffs on six occasions though they didn't have much success and were eliminated in their first round on all six.

15. In what year of their existence as an NHL franchise did the Winnipeg Jets make the Stanley Cup playoffs?
a) Third   b) Fourth   c) Fifth   d) Sixth

   a) Third. The Winnipeg Jets qualified for the Stanley Cup playoffs for the first time in the 1981–82 season but lost that series three games to one to the St. Louis Blues.

16. In 1985, the NHL conducted its first Entry Draft outside Montreal. Where did the 1985 draft occur?
a) Buffalo   b) Detroit   c) Toronto   d) Vancouver

c) Toronto. The Toronto Convention Centre was host to the NHL Entry Draft on June 15, 1985, marking the first time it had been held outside Montreal. Wendel Clark was chosen first overall by the hometown Leafs in this draft.

17. How many points did Mario Lemieux record in his first NHL season?
a) 76   b) 95   c) 100   d) 141

c) 100. Mario Lemieux recorded 43 goals and 57 assists for 100 points in 73 games during his rookie season of 1984–85. He earned 76 points in 43 games when he came back to the NHL for 2000–2001.

18. Which of the following players recorded the best plus-minus in a single NHL season (though none equaled Bobby Orr's plus 124 goal differential of 1970–71)?
a) Ray Bourque   b) Wayne Gretzky
c) Mario Lemieux   d) Mark Messier

b) Wayne Gretzky.

Best Plus-Minus Season

Wayne Gretzky	Edmonton	1984–85	+98
Mario Lemieux	Pittsburgh	1992–93	+55
Ray Bourque	Boston	1979–80	+52
Mark Messier	Edmonton	1983–84	+40

19. When was the last time that a best-of-five format was used for a playoff in the NHL?
a) 1980   b) 1982   c) 1984   d) 1986

d) 1986. The first round of the Stanley Cup playoffs was a best-of-five series from 1980 to 1986, but all series have been played in the best-of-seven format since then.

20. Who holds the record for the most shorthanded goals in one NHL season?
a) Marcel Dionne   b) Wayne Gretzky
c) Dirk Graham   d) Mario Lemieux

Wayne Gretzky was awarded the Hart Trophy as league MVP in each of his first eight NHL seasons.

d) Mario Lemieux.

Most Shorthanded Goals in an NHL Season

Mario Lemieux	Pittsburgh	1988–89	13
		1987–88	10
Wayne Gretzky	Edmonton	1983–84	12
		1984–85	11
Marcel Dionne	Detroit	1974–75	10
Dirk Graham	Chicago	1988–89	10

Third Period: Expert Trivia

1. Name the four members of the 1986 Stanley Cup champion Montreal Canadiens who had brothers who had also played or would play in the NHL. (Hint: The non-Cup-winning brothers were Dan, Jocelyn, Moe and Stephane.)

John Kordic, Claude Lemieux, Larry Robinson and Patrick Roy were all members of the 1986 Cup-winning Canadiens who had brothers who played in the NHL. Kordic's brother Dan played 197 regular-season and 12 playoff games with Philadelphia between 1991 and 1999. Claude Lemieux's brother Jocelyn played a total of 598 regular-season and 60 playoff games with seven different NHL franchises from 1986 to 1998. Larry Robinson's brother Moe played a single game for the Montreal Canadiens in the 1979–80 season and Patrick Roy's brother Stephane played 12 games for the Minnesota North Stars in 1987–88.

2. Name the three captains of the Calgary Flames during their Stanley Cup championship season of 1988–89.

Lanny McDonald, Jim Peplinski and Tim Hunter.

3. The four surviving WHA teams were accepted into the NHL as expansion franchises in the 1979–80 season. Which was the first team to select first overall in the Entry Draft and who did they select?

The Winnipeg Jets received the first overall Entry Draft pick in 1981 and they chose Dale Hawerchuk from the Cornwall Royals.

4. There have been only two all-Canadian Stanley Cup finals since the NHL expanded in 1967. When were they?

The only two all-Canadian Stanley Cup finals since Toronto and Montreal faced off in the Original Six era in 1967 were in 1986 and 1989. In both cases, the Calgary Flames and the Montreal Canadiens faced off in the finals.

5. Name the only two players other than Phil Esposito, Wayne Gretzky and Mario Lemieux to record 150 or more points in a single NHL season.

Steve Yzerman and Bernie Nicholls. In 1988–89, Yzerman recorded 65 goals and 90 assists for 155 points with the Detroit Red Wings and Nicholls recorded 70 goals and 80 assists for 150 points with the Los Angeles Kings.

6. An NHL franchise has selected the first overall pick in the Entry Draft three consecutive times only once. Name this team and the players selected.

The Quebec Nordiques held the first overall pick for three consecutive years. In 1989, they selected Mats Sundin first overall, in 1990 they selected Owen Nolan and the following year they selected Eric Lindros.

7. Name the two individuals who have scored 50 or more goals in a single NHL season as a member of two different teams.

Craig Simpson and Dave Andreychuk. Simpson recorded 13 goals in 21 games for the Penguins and 43 goals in 59 games with the Oilers for a total of 56 goals in 1987–88. Andreychuk scored 29 goals in 52 games for the Sabres and added 25 more in 31 games with the Leafs for a total of 54 goals in 1992–93.

8. Name the three NHL goalies who saw action with Team Canada in the 1984 Canada Cup.

Grant Fuhr, Reggie Lemelin and Pete Peeters. Grant Fuhr of the Edmonton Oilers started the 1984 Canada Cup but was injured early in the tournament. Pete Peeters of the Boston Bruins and Reggie Lemelin of the Calgary Flames played the remainder of the tournament, through to Canada's victory over Sweden in the finals.

9. Mario Lemieux played his first NHL regular-season game in October 1984. When did he first play in a playoff game?

The Penguins didn't reach the Stanley Cup playoffs until Mario's fifth season in Pittsburgh. He played his first playoff game on April 5, 1989, a 3–1 Pittsburgh victory over the New York Rangers in the division semifinals. They went on to sweep the Rangers four games straight but failed to advance beyond the division finals against Philadelphia. In spite of Mario's outstanding performance (he recorded 12 goals and seven assists for 19 points in 11 playoff games), they lost the series four games to three. After missing the playoffs for a fifth time in 1989–90, Mario led the Penguins to their first Stanley Cup victory in 1991.

10. Name the only two non-goalies to win the Calder Trophy and be selected to the NHL's First All–Star Team in their rookie season.

Ray Bourque and Teemu Selanne. Bourque captured both of these honors as a Bruin in 1979–80. He played in all of Boston's 80 games, recording 17 goals and 48 assists for 65 points in an outstanding plus 52 for the season. This was also Wayne Gretzky's first season in the NHL, but he'd been declared ineligible for the Calder Trophy because he'd already played professionally in the WHA. He finished second to Marcel Dionne for center in the All–Star voting.

Teemu Selanne exploded on to the NHL scene with the Winnipeg Jets in 1992–93. He scored a record 76 goals as a rookie and finished fifth in the NHL scoring race with 132 points, both feats no other rookie has come close to duplicating.

11. None of the "Big Three" completed their NHL playing career as Montreal Canadiens. Where did Guy Lapointe, Larry Robinson and Serge Savard each play their last NHL season?

Guy Lapointe played his final NHL season as a Boston Bruin in 1983–84. He also saw action with the St. Louis Blues after his outstanding career with the Montreal Canadiens. Larry Robinson played his final three seasons as a member of the Los Angeles Kings, retiring at the end of the 1991–92 season. Serge Savard played two seasons on defense for the Winnipeg Jets, completing his NHL playing career in 1982–83.

12. When Wayne Gretzky was traded to Los Angeles by Edmonton on August 9, 1988, there were four other players involved. How many can you name?

Mike Krushelnyski and Marty McSorley accompanied Wayne Gretzky to Los Angeles, while Edmonton received Jimmy Carson, Martin Gelinas—Los Angeles' first-round choices in the Entry Drafts of 1989, 1991 and 1993—and cash.

13. When the four ex-WHA franchises joined the NHL in 1979, they were allowed to protect up to four players from their previous year's roster from being reclaimed by the existing teams. Name the three players who were protected by the Edmonton Oilers and went on to play with the club in the 1979–80 NHL season.

Wayne Gretzky and goaltenders Dave Dryden and Eddie Mio were protected by Edmonton in 1979.

14. Two of the NHL's all-time greatest defensemen made the same switch in their sweater numbers during the 1987–88 season. Can you name the players and explain their decision?

Both Ray Bourque and Paul Coffey switched from number 7 to number 77 in 1987–88. Bourque was into his ninth season as a member of the Bruins and was wearing number 7 when they honored Phil Esposito on December 3, 1987. He revealed his new number, 77, when he removed his number 7 sweater and handed it to Esposito as the Bruins retired the number to honor Phil's contributions to the franchise. Paul Coffey wore number 7 for his first seven NHL seasons with the Edmonton Oilers. Following a contract dispute with the Oilers, Coffey was traded to the Pittsburgh Penguins in November 1988. When Coffey arrived in Pittsburgh, Rod Buskas wore number 7, so Coffey took number 77.

15. What sweater number did Joe Sakic wear during his NHL rookie season?

Joe Sakic wore number 88 with the Quebec Nordiques for the 1988–89 season. He switched to his present number (19) for his second season in the NHL.

16. Where did former Toronto captain Darryl Sittler finish his NHL playing career?

Darryl Sittler's final NHL action was with the Detroit Red Wings in 1984–85.

17. Where did Mario Lemieux play his final game of junior hockey?

Kitchener, Ontario. Lemieux's final amateur appearance was as a member of the Laval Titans of the Quebec Major Junior Hockey League when they competed in the 1984 Memorial Cup tournament held in Kitchener, Ontario, in May. Laval's final game of the tournament was a 4–3 round-robin loss to the Kamloops Oilers. Lemieux had recorded an amazing 282 points in 70 regular-season games with Laval and would go on to be selected number one overall by the Pittsburgh Penguins in the NHL Entry Draft the following month.

18. The Washington Capitals traded Rick Green and Ryan Walter to the Montreal Canadiens in September 1982. Name the four players the Caps received in return.

Brian Engblom, Rod Langway, Doug Jarvis and Craig Laughlin went to Washington from Montreal in 1982.

19. Name the last player to be chosen first overall in the NHL Entry Draft by the Montreal Canadiens.

Doug Wickenheiser of the Regina Pats was selected first overall by the Montreal Canadiens in the 1980 Entry Draft, followed by Dave Babych (Winnipeg), Denis Savard (Chicago), Larry Murphy (Los Angeles), Darren Veitch (Washington) and Paul Coffey (Edmonton).

20. The King Clancy Memorial Trophy has been awarded since 1988 to the player who best demonstrates leadership and humanitarian contribution to the community. Who was the first recipient of this award?

Lanny McDonald of the Calgary Flames was the first player to receive the King Clancy Memorial Trophy.

Overtime: Four on Four

1. Name the four members of the New York Islanders who were Conn Smythe Trophy winners during their four Stanley Cup seasons.

Bryan Trottier won the Conn Smythe Trophy in 1980, Butch Goring in 1981, Mike Bossy in 1982 and Billy Smith in 1983.

2. **Name the only four individuals to captain and later coach the St. Louis Blues.**

Al Arbour, Red Berenson, Barclay Plager and Brian Sutter. Al Arbour was captain of the St. Louis Blues from 1967–68 to 1969–70 and would go on to a lengthy career coaching for St. Louis in portions of 1970–71, 1971–72 and 1972–73. He also coached the New York Islanders for 19 NHL seasons between 1973–74 and 1993–94. Red Berenson was captain of the Blues during part of 1970–71 and all of 1977–78. He went on to coach St. Louis during 1979–80 and in to the 1981–82 season. Barclay Plager was the Blues' captain from the 1970–71 season to the end of 1975–76 and coached St. Louis during portions of four different seasons, 1977–78 through 1979–80 and again in 1982–83. Brian Sutter served as the team captain from 1979–80 to 1987–88 and took over as the coach from 1988–89 to 1991–92. Sutter has since coached both the Boston Bruins and the Calgary Flames. He has also been named Chicago's coach for the 2001–02 season.

3. **Wayne Gretzky is the only individual to record 200 or more points in a single NHL season—and he did it four times. Identify the four seasons and Gretzky's point totals during each.**

Wayne Gretzky—200-Plus Points Seasons

	GP	G	A	PTS
1985–86	80	52	163	215
1981–82	80	92	120	212
1984–85	80	73	135	208
1983–84	74	87	118	205

4. **Name the only four players to score four goals in a single NHL All–Star Game.**

Wayne Gretzky scored four goals in the 1983 All–Star Game, followed by Mario Lemieux (1990), Vincent Damphousse (1991) and Mike Gartner (1993).

Game 7: Heading South

1993 to 2001

The 1990s brought further expansion as the NHL reached 30 teams with the addition of the Columbus Blue Jackets and Minnesota Wild for the 2000–2001 season. A massive influx of European talent helped build the rosters of so many big-league teams, while franchises shifted south when a falling Canadian dollar created difficulties for teams in Canadian cities. The Stanley Cup also seemed to be heading south, with the 1992–93 Montreal Canadiens being the last to take it to a Canadian city after the post-season. We all said our goodbyes to Wayne and Mario, but both have remained active in the game, and Mario even returned as a player midway through 2000–2001.

First Period: Who Am I?

1. I am the first player to take two penalty shots during the same Stanley Cup playoff year.

Mats Sundin of the Toronto Maple Leafs was awarded two penalty shots during the 1999 playoffs. On April 22, he was stopped by John Vanbiesbrouck of the Philadelphia Flyers in a 3–0 win by Philadelphia. On May 29, he scored on Dominik Hasek of the Buffalo Sabres, but Buffalo won the game 5–2.

2. I am the most recent winner of back-to-back Hart awards as the NHL's most valuable player in the regular season.

Dominik Hasek won the Hart Trophy in both 1997 and 1998.

3. I was the only Canadian-born captain of an NHL franchise based in Canada at the close of the 2000–2001 season.

Dave Lowry, a native of Sudbury, Ontario, was the only Canadian-born captain among the six NHL franchises based in Canada at the close of the 2000–2001 season. Swedish-born Daniel Alfredsson, Mats Sundin and Markus Naslund captained Ottawa, Toronto and Vancouver respectively, while Finnish-born Saku Koivu led Montreal and American-born Doug Weight led Edmonton during the season.

4. I was the first captain of the Atlanta Thrashers. (Hint: I had been the captain of another NHL franchise for the four previous seasons.)

Kelly Buchberger was the first captain of the Atlanta Thrashers in the 1999–2000 season before being traded to Los Angeles on March 13, 2000. Buchberger had previously been the captain of the Edmonton Oilers, from 1995 to 1999.

5. I recorded a team-leading 30 goals with the Columbus Blue Jackets in their inaugural season of 2000–2001.

Geoff Sanderson regained his scoring touch as a member of the Columbus Blue Jackets, reaching the 30-goal plateau for the fifth time in 2000–2001.

6. I was the last coach of the Winnipeg Jets.

Terry Simpson took on his third coaching job (he had previously coached with the New York Islanders and Philadelphia Flyers) when he took over the Winnipeg Jets near the end of the 1994–95 season and coached them through the end of the 1995–96 regular season and playoffs. He was replaced by Don Hay when the Jets relocated to Phoenix as the Coyotes for 1996–97.

7. I played goal for six different NHL teams between 1972 and 1985 and I've since been the head coach for two different NHL franchises.

Ron Low played goal with the Toronto Maple Leafs in 1972–73 and saw stops in Washington, Detroit, Quebec, Edmonton and New Jersey before retiring after the 1984–85 season. He was head coach of the Edmonton Oilers from 1995 through 1999 and the New York Rangers for the 2000–2001 season.

8. I am the only player ever to score in a fifth overtime period in the Stanley Cup playoffs.

Keith Primeau scored at 12:01 of the fifth overtime period in a conference semifinal game when Philadelphia defeated Pittsburgh 2–1 on May 4, 2000.

9. I was the first captain of the Anaheim Mighty Ducks. (Hint: I was a member of the Pittsburgh Penguins Stanley Cup teams in 1990–91 and 1991–92.)

Troy Loney had played 10 seasons with the Pittsburgh Penguins when he was selected by Anaheim in the 1993 Expansion Draft. He was captain of the Mighty Ducks in their first—and his only—season in Anaheim, 1993–94. He was then traded to the New York Islanders and finished his NHL career with the New York Rangers in 1994–95.

10. I followed in my father's footsteps when I became a head coach for the 1999–2000 NHL season.

Bobby Francis became head coach of the Phoenix Coyotes for the 1999–2000 season. Emile Francis had been an NHL netminder with Chicago and New York in the late 1940s and early 1950s and went on to become a successful NHL coach with both the New York Rangers and the St. Louis Blues. Bobby had a successful minor-league career and saw NHL action in 14 games with the Detroit Red Wings in 1982–83.

11. I was a double trophy winner in 1995, taking home both the Lady Byng and Frank J. Selke awards.

Ron Francis of the Pittsburgh Penguins won his first Selke Trophy as the NHL's outstanding defensive forward and his first Lady Byng as the league's most gentlemanly and skilled player in 1995. Francis won a second Lady Byng Trophy in 1998, still with the Penguins, before moving on to the Carolina Hurricanes the following season.

12. I retired at the end of the 1999–2000 season as a three-time winner of the Selke Trophy as the NHL's best defensive forward and a member of three Cup-winning teams.

Guy Carbonneau won the Cup three times, twice with the Montreal Canadiens (in 1986 and 1993) and again in 1999 with the Dallas Stars. He won the Selke Trophy as the NHL's best defensive forward in 1988, 1989 and 1992. He played one season in St. Louis (1994–95) before moving on to the Dallas Stars in 1995–96, when the Stars missed the playoffs—the only time during his career that he didn't take part in the post-season.

13. I am the last player to record back-to-back seasons of 60 goals or more.

Pavel Bure recorded back-to-back 60-goal seasons during 1992–93 and 1993–94 with the Vancouver Canucks.

14. Montreal traded me to the Philadelphia Flyers along with Eric Desjardins and John LeClair for Mike Recchi and a third-round draft choice in February 1995. (Hint: My brother is a member of the Hockey Hall of Fame.)

Gilbert Dionne played in 196 games with the Montreal Canadiens before the trade. He took part in only 22 games as a Flyer before moving on for five more with the Florida Panthers in 1995–96. Gilbert's brother is Hall of Famer Marcel Dionne.

15. I lead active NHL players in regular-season games played with only one franchise.

Steve Yzerman has played all 18 seasons of his NHL career (from 1983–84 through to the end of the 2000–2001 season) with the Detroit Red Wings—1,310 regular-season games.

16. I'm the last player who wasn't the captain of my team when I won the Art Ross Trophy as the NHL's leading scorer.

Jaromir Jagr won the Art Ross Trophy as the NHL's leading scorer in 1997–98, when Ron Francis was serving as captain of the Pittsburgh Penguins.

17. I've led the Nashville Predators' scoring in each of their first three seasons.

Cliff Ronning. While Ronning was traded from Phoenix in late October of the Predators' first season, he still managed to record enough points in Nashville's remaining games to be the club's scoring leader. He has gone on to lead the club in scoring in the two subsequent seasons.

	GP	G	A	PTS
1998–1999	72	18	35	53
1999–2000	82	26	36	62
2000–2001	80	19	43	62

18. I was captain in three different NHL cities over a span of five seasons. (Hint: I was the captain of the Philadelphia Flyers prior to Eric Lindros.)

Kevin Dineen was the captain of the Philadelphia Flyers for the 1993–94 season, the Hartford Whalers in 1996–97 and the relocated Carolina Hurricanes in 1997–98.

19. I was the leading scorer for the Anaheim Mighty Ducks in their first NHL season.

Terry Yake had been claimed from the Hartford Whalers in the 1993 Expansion Draft. He scored 21 goals and added 31 assists for 52 points to be the club's leading scorer in his only season with the franchise. He was traded to the Maple Leafs before the 1994–95 season.

20. My 10 shutouts in 2000–2001 were the most by a first-year goaltender in more than 30 seasons.

Roman Cechmanek recorded 10 shutouts in his first NHL season as a member of the Philadelphia Flyers in 2000–2001. Tony Esposito had recorded 15 for the Chicago Black Hawks in his first full season in the NHL, 1969–70.

Second Period: Multiple Choice

1. How many times has a Canadian-based NHL franchise made the Stanley Cup finals since Montreal won in 1993?
a) 0   b) 1   c) 2   d) 3

b) 1. Since 1993, the single appearance of a Canadian-based franchise was made by the Vancouver Canucks, who played in the 1994 Stanley Cup finals and lost to the New York Rangers in a seven-game series.

2. How many times has Dominik Hasek won the Vezina Trophy?
a) 3   b) 4   c) 5   d) 6

d) 6. Hasek won the Vezina Trophy as the NHL's outstanding goaltender in 1994, 1995, 1997, 1998, 1999 and 2001.

3. Mike Keenan had been head coach of how many different NHL teams by the end of the 2000–2001 season?
a) 4   b) 5   c) 6   d) 7

c) 6. Keenan has been head coach in Philadelphia, Chicago, New York (with the Rangers), St. Louis, Vancouver and Boston.

4. How many members of the 2000–2001 New York Rangers had also won the Cup in 1994?
a) 2   b) 3   c) 4   d) 5

c) 4. Goaltender Mike Richter, defenseman Brian Leetch, forwards Adam Graves and Mark Messier were all members of both New York teams. Mark Messier spent three of the intervening seasons with the Vancouver Canucks but returned to the Rangers for 2000–2001.

5. Of all the players selected in the first 32 universal amateur/entry drafts conducted by the NHL from 1969 through 2000, how many have never suited up for the team that selected them as number one overall in the draft?
a) 1   b) 2   c) 3   d) 4

b) 2. Eric Lindros was the first selection (by the Quebec Nordiques) in 1991 and Bryan Berard was the first selection (of the Ottawa Senators) in 1995—the only two individuals picked number one overall never to suit up with the team that selected them.

6. How many Stanley Cup playoff game victories have been recorded by the Tampa Bay Lightning?
a) 0   b) 1   c) 2   d) 3

c) 2. The only playoff games the Tampa Bay Lightning have ever won were both overtime victories in the 1996 conference quarterfinals against the Philadelphia Flyers. Tampa won game two on April 18, 1996, when Brian Bellows scored at 9:05 of overtime to give his team a 2–1 win over Philadelphia and Alexander Selivanov scored at 2:04 of overtime of game three on April 21, 1996, to give Tampa a 5–4 win. Philadelphia went on to win the next three games to take the series in Tampa Bay's lone Stanley Cup series appearance.

7. The Anaheim Mighty Ducks have advanced beyond the first series of the Stanley Cup playoffs only once. What team did they defeat?
a) The Detroit Red Wings   b) The Los Angeles Kings
c) The Phoenix Coyotes   d) The San Jose Sharks

c) The Phoenix Coyotes. Anaheim defeated Phoenix four games to three in the conference quarterfinals before being eliminated by Detroit in four straight games in the semifinals. During the only other time that Anaheim has advanced to the playoffs, they were swept in four straight games in the conference quarter finals by the Detroit Red Wings in 1999.

8. When was the last time a player recorded 60 goals in an NHL season?
a) 1993–94   b) 1995–96   c) 1996–97   d) 2000–2001

b) 1995–96. Mario Lemieux and Jaromir Jagr recorded 69 and 62 goals respectively in 1995–96.

9. How many players who saw action as Minnesota North Stars were still with the franchise as Dallas Stars at the conclusion of the 2000–2001 season?
a) 1   b) 2   c) 3   d) 4

c) 3. Richard Matvichuk was a rookie in 1992–93—the Stars' last season in Minnesota—and he suited up for 53 games on Minnesota's defense. Mike Modano played his first two games with the North Stars in the 1989 Stanley Cup playoffs and has been a regular since the 1989–90 season, having played four full seasons in Minnesota before the franchise relocated to Dallas. Derian Hatcher has been on defense with the franchise since 1991–92.

10. Who has been the head coach of the highest number of NHL franchises at the end of the 2000–2001 season?
a) Scotty Bowman   b) Jacques Demers
c) Mike Keenan   d) Roger Neilson

d) Roger Neilson was head coach of a record seven NHL franchises—Toronto, Buffalo, Vancouver, Los Angeles, the New York Rangers, Florida and Philadelphia—between 1977 and 2000. Mike Keenan finished the 2000–2001 season as head coach of his sixth NHL franchise. Keenan has coached Philadelphia, Chicago, the New York Rangers, St. Louis, Vancouver and Boston between 1984 and 2001. Both Scotty Bowman and Jacques Demers have been head coaches on five different NHL teams, Bowman with St. Louis, Montreal, Buffalo, Pittsburgh and Detroit between 1967 and 2001 and Demers with Quebec, St. Louis, Detroit, Montreal and Tampa Bay between 1979 and 1999.

11. What is the lowest number of Original Six franchises to qualify for the Stanley Cup playoffs in a given year?
a) 1   b) 2   c) 3   d) 4

b) 2. The 1999–2000 season marked the first time that as few as two teams of the Original Six franchises qualified for the Stanley Cup playoffs since 1926–27, when Chicago, Detroit and New York entered the league. The Boston Bruins, Chicago Blackhawks, Montreal Canadiens and New York Rangers all missed the playoffs for the second consecutive season in 2000–2001.

12. Which player was never the captain of the Montreal Canadiens?
a) Mike Keane   b) Kirk Muller
c) Brian Skrudland   d) Pierre Turgeon

c) Brian Skrudland. While Skrudland served as captain of the Florida Panthers from 1993 to 1997, he was never appointed captain of the Montreal Canadiens. Kirk Muller was the captain of the Canadiens for the first half of the 1994–95 season, until he was traded to the New York Islanders, when Mike Keane took over. Keane remained captain until midway through the following season, when he was traded to the Colorado Avalanche. Pierre Turgeon—who the Canadiens had received in the Kirk Muller trade—then served as captain until early in the 1996–97 season, when he was traded to St. Louis.

13. How many NHL clubs have retired number 18?
a) 1   b) 2   c) 3   d) 4

b) 2. Both the Chicago Blackhawks and the Los Angeles Kings have retired number 18. Chicago retired the number to honor fan favorite Denis Savard, who played for the Hawks for his first 10 seasons in the NHL, beginning in 1980–81. Savard went on to play with the Montreal Canadiens and Tampa Bay Lightning before returning to the Blackhawks during the 1994–95 season and he finished his playing career there at the end of the 1996–97 season. The Los Angeles Kings retired number 18 to honor Dave Taylor, who played his entire 17-year NHL career (from 1977 through 1994) with the Kings.

14. As of the end of the 2000–2001 season, which of the following franchises has experienced the longest stretch without winning a Stanley Cup playoff series?

Mario Lemieux amazed hockey fans again with his successful return during the 2000-2001 season.

a) The Calgary Flames   b) The Carolina Hurricanes
c) The New York Islanders   d) The Phoenix Coyotes

    b) The Carolina Hurricanes last won a playoff series as the Hartford Whalers in the 1986 playoffs. Hartford defeated the Quebec Nordiques three games to none in the division semifinals before being eliminated by the Montreal Canadiens in seven games in the division finals. The Phoenix Coyotes franchise hasn't won a playoff series since, as the Winnipeg Jets, they defeated Calgary four games to two in the 1987 division semifinals. The Calgary Flames haven't won since their Cup victory in 1989. The New York Islanders last won a playoff series in 1993, when they eliminated Pittsburgh four games to three in the division finals before being ousted by Montreal in the conference finals.

15. Wayne Gretzky, Mario Lemieux and Jaromir Jagr were the only players to win the Art Ross Trophy in the 21 seasons from 1980–81 to 2000–2001. How many players placed second in the NHL regular-season scoring race during that time?
a) 9   b) 12   c) 15   d) 18

    d) 18. Gretzky, Jari Kurri and Teemu Selanne have all been runner-ups for the Art Ross Trophy on two occasions during these 21 seasons. Another 15 players—including Lemieux and Jagr—have finished second in scoring during one of them.

16. The following players were all selected by the Ottawa Senators in the Entry Draft. Which wasn't a number one pick overall?
a) Bryan Berard   b) Alexandre Daigle
c) Chris Phillips   d) Alexei Yashin

    d) Alexei Yashin was chosen second overall in the 1992 Entry Draft, after Roman Hamrlik, who was chosen by the Tampa Bay Lightning. Daigle was the first selection by Ottawa in 1993. Bryan Berard was selected first overall in 1995 but never played a game with the Senators, as he was included in a multiple-player trade to the New York Islanders that brought Wade Redden back to Ottawa. Chris Phillips was the number one pick overall in the 1996 draft.

17. What was the most common country of origin among the top 10 scorers for the 2000–2001 NHL regular season?
a) Canada   b) Czech Republic
c) Russia   d) Sweden

b) Czech Republic. Three of the top 10 scorers in the 2000–2001 NHL season are natives of the Czech Republic.

	G	A	PTS	Country of Origin
Jaromir Jagr (Pittsburgh)	52	69	121	Czech Republic
Joe Sakic (Colorado)	54	64	118	Canada
Patrik Elias (New Jersey)	40	56	96	Czech Republic
Alexei Kovalev (Pittsburgh)	44	51	95	Russia
Jason Allison (Boston)	36	59	95	Canada
Martin Straka (Pittsburgh)	27	68	95	Czech Republic
Pavel Bure (Florida)	59	33	92	Russia
Doug Weight (Edmonton)	25	65	90	United States
Zigmund Palffy (Los Angeles)	38	51	89	Slovakia
Peter Forsberg (Colorado)	27	62	89	Sweden

18. How many of the 30 franchises currently in the NHL have never competed in a Stanley Cup final series?
a) 7   b) 8   c) 9   d) 10

d) 10. Of the 13 teams that have joined the NHL since 1979, only Edmonton, Quebec/Colorado and Florida have advanced to the Stanley Cup finals.

NHL Franchises Who Have Not Played in a Stanley Cup Final

Team	First NHL Season
Hartford/Carolina	1979–80
Winnipeg/Phoenix	1979–80
San Jose	1991–92
Ottawa	1992–93
Tampa Bay	1992–93
Anaheim	1993–94
Nashville	1998–99
Atlanta	1999–2000
Columbus	2000–2001
Minnesota	2000–2001

19. How many of the NHL's now 30 franchises have relocated to a new city at some point in their existence?
a) 6   b) 7   c) 8   d) 9

a) 6. NHL franchises at present located in Calgary, Carolina, Colorado, Dallas, New Jersey and Phoenix have all been relocated at some point.

20. Which of the following cities has never had an NHL franchise?
a) Cleveland   b) Hamilton   c) Kansas City   d) Seattle

d) Seattle. The Hamilton Tigers played from 1920 to 1925, the Kansas City Scouts from 1974 to 1976 and the Cleveland Barons from 1976 to 1978.

Third Period: Expert Trivia

1. **When was the first time an NHL All-Star Game didn't include a Montreal Canadien?**
In the 2001 All-Star Game in Denver, Colorado, there were no Montreal Canadiens on either the North American or World team.

2. **What is the connection between Ottawa's first selection in the Entry Draft of 1995 and 1997?**
Ottawa's first selection in the 1995 draft, Bryan Berard (first overall), played his last NHL game on March 11, 2000, when Ottawa's first selection in the 1997 Entry Draft, Marian Hossa (12th overall), caught his eye with a stick, which ultimately led to Berard's retirement from NHL hockey.

3. **General manager Bob Gainey, himself a former Canadien captain, had three former Montreal captains on his Dallas Stars for the 2000 Stanley Cup finals. Name them.**
Guy Carbonneau was captain of the Canadiens from 1989–90 through 1993–94, Kirk Muller took over in 1994–95 and Mike Keane led the team in 1994–95 and 1995–96.

4. **Name the only two pre-1996 number one overall picks in the Entry Draft who were still playing with the same franchise at the end of the 2000–2001 season.**
Mario Lemieux was chosen by the Pittsburgh Penguins in the 1984 Entry Draft and Mike Modano was chosen by the Minnesota North Stars (now Dallas Stars) in 1988.

5. **A defenseman has been the number one overall selection for three consecutive years in only one sequence of Entry Drafts. When did this happen and who were the three defensemen?**

In 1994, Ed Jovanovski was chosen by the Florida Panthers, followed by Bryan Berard in 1995 and Chris Phillips in 1996, both chosen by the Ottawa Senators.

6. Name the two players who closed the 2000–2001 season with the Phoenix Coyotes who had been with the club continuously since the franchise was known as the Winnipeg Jets.

Teppo Numminen and Shane Doan. Numminen has been a regular on the Winnipeg/Phoenix defense since 1988–89, while Doan's rookie season was the last before the relocation, 1995–96.

7. Name the only three players to score for the Philadelphia Flyers during the 1997 Stanley Cup finals against the Detroit Red Wings.

Rod Brind'Amour, John LeClair and Eric Lindros. Brind'Amour scored three, John LeClair two and Eric Lindros a single goal as the Flyers recorded only six goals during the 1997 Stanley Cup finals, when they were swept by the Red Wings in four straight games.

8. Name the only season in NHL history when the eight leading scorers all came from different NHL clubs.

In 1993–94, the scoring race finished with Wayne Gretzky (Los Angeles Kings) at 130 points; Sergei Fedorov (Detroit Red Wings) at 120; Adam Oates (Boston Bruins) at 112; Doug Gilmour (Toronto Maple Leafs) at 111; Pavel Bure (Vancouver Canucks) at 107; Jeremy Roenick (Chicago Blackhawks) at 107; Mike Recchi (Philadelphia Flyers) at 107; and Brendan Shanahan (St. Louis Blues) at 102.

9. Name the three former captains of an NHL team who were general manager of that franchise at the end of the 2000–2001 season.

Bobby Clarke, Kevin Lowe and Dave Taylor. Philadelphia GM Bobby Clarke served as captain of the team from 1972–73 through the end of 1978–79 and again in 1982–83 and 1983–84. Edmonton GM Kevin Lowe served as captain during the 1991–92 season. Los Angeles GM Dave Taylor served as the Kings' captain from 1985–86 to 1988–89.

10. Name the only two NHL seasons since 1969–70 when no one scored 50 goals.

The 1994–95 season was shortened by a lockout that resulted in a 48-game NHL year. In 1998–99, the Maurice "Rocket" Richard Trophy was awarded for the first time and Teemu Selanne of the Anaheim Mighty Ducks was the leading scorer with 47 goals.

11. Name the two players who were members of the 1993 Stanley Cup Montreal Canadiens who were still Canadiens at the end of the 2000–2001 season.

Defenseman Patrice Brisebois and left winger Benoit Brunet were the only players from the 1993 Stanley Cup team still playing for the Montreal Canadiens at the end of the 2000–2001 season.

12. Name the first three European-trained players to be selected number one overall in the NHL Entry Draft.

Mats Sundin, Roman Hamrlik and Patrik Stefan. Mats Sundin of Sweden was selected first overall in 1989 by the Quebec Nordiques, Roman Hamrlik of the Czech Republic was chosen first overall by the Tampa Bay Lightning in 1992 and Patrik Stefan, also of the Czech Republic, was chosen first overall by the Atlanta Thrashers in the 1999 draft.

13. Philadelphia Flyers general manager Bobby Clarke has held a similar post with what two other NHL franchises?

The Minnesota North Stars and the Florida Panthers. Clarke was the general manager in Philadelphia from 1984–85 to 1989–90 and left to become GM of the Minnesota North Stars (now the Dallas Stars) for 1990–91 and 1991–92. He then became the first GM for the Florida Panthers for 1993–94 and returned to the Flyers in 1994–95 and has served there till the time of this writing.

14. Colin Campbell, the NHL's executive vice-president and director of hockey operations, also had an 11-year career in the league as a player before becoming a coach and now vice-president. Name the five NHL teams Campbell played for in his NHL career.

The Pittsburgh Penguins, Colorado Rockies, Edmonton Oilers, Vancouver Canucks and Detroit Red Wings. Campbell played the 1973–74 season with the Vancouver Blazers of the WHA before entering the NHL with the Pittsburgh Penguins in 1974–75 and 1975–76. He spent 1976–77 in Colorado, then went back to Pittsburgh for 1977–78 and 1978–79. He played 1979–80 with the Edmonton Oilers, 1980–81 and 1981–82 with the Canucks—where he made his only trip to the Stanley Cup finals in 1982—and played his last three seasons in the NHL with the Red Wings between 1982–83 and 1984–85.

15. Name the three players who represented the Maple Leafs at the 2000 All–Star Game in Toronto.

Curtis Joseph (North America); Mats Sundin and Dimitry Yushkevish (World). The World All–Stars defeated North America All–Stars 9–4.

16. Name the two ex-NHL netminders who were general managers of NHL teams at the end of the 2000–2001 season.

Ken Holland of the Detroit Red Wings and Jim Rutherford of the Carolina Hurricanes. Detroit GM Ken Holland played one game in goal for the Hartford Whalers during the 1980–81 season and three for the Red Wings in 1983–84 (the rookie year for Holland's current Detroit captain, Steve Yzerman). Jim Rutherford played for the Detroit Red Wings, Pittsburgh Penguins, Toronto Maple Leafs and Los Angeles Kings between 1970 and 1982.

17. Name the two former members of the Edmonton Oilers who scored Stanley Cup-winning goals with other franchises.

Mark Messier and Jason Arnott. Messier scored the Cup-winning goal for the New York Rangers in 1994 and Arnott scored the clincher in 2000 for the New Jersey Devils.

18. Name the only three individuals who have played with the Florida Panthers during all of the team's first eight seasons in the NHL (1993–94 to 2000–2001.)

Paul Laus, Scott Mellanby and Rod Niedermayer have been with the Panthers since 1993–94. Scott Mellanby was traded to the St. Louis Blues during the 2000–2001 season, but both Laus and Niedermayer closed the season still members of the Florida Panthers.

19. In which province or state are the most NHL teams located?

Both California (Anaheim, Los Angeles, San Jose) and New York State (Buffalo, Islanders, Rangers) have three NHL franchises.

20. Name the two rookies who led their teams in scoring in 2000–2001.

Marian Gaborik had a team-leading 36 points with the Minnesota Wild, while Brad Richards recorded 62 points to lead Tampa Bay in scoring during the 2000–2001 season.

Overtime: Four on Four

1. When Cliff Fletcher became general manager of the Phoenix Coyotes during the 2000–2001 season, he was only the fifth GM in the history of the Winnipeg/Phoenix franchise. Name the previous four.

John Ferguson was the general manager from 1979–80 until he was replaced by Mike Smith in 1988–89. Smith was replaced by John Paddock in 1993–94 and Bobby Smith took over in 1996–97. Cliff Fletcher took over from Smith in 2000–2001.

2. The Detroit Red Wings finally ended a 32-year drought with their Stanley Cup victory in 1997. Name the four teams Detroit defeated en route to winning their first Cup since 1955.

Detroit defeated St. Louis four games to two in the conference quarterfinals before going on to sweep Anaheim in four straight games in the conference semis. Then they beat Colorado in a spirited six-game series before sweeping the Philadelphia Flyers in four straight to take the Cup title.

3. Name the four individuals who have been captain of their team for the longest continuous time and were still serving in that capacity at the end of the 2000–2001 season.

Steve Yzerman has captained the Detroit Red Wings since 1986–87, Joe Sakic has led the Quebec Nordiques/Colorado Avalanche since 1992–93, Scott Stevens has been at the helm for the New Jersey Devils since 1992–93, Derian Hatcher has worn the "C" on the Dallas Stars since 1995–96 and all were still serving as captains at the end of 2000–2001.

4. Name the four active NHL goalies who have played all of their 300-plus regular-season games with a single team.

Mike Richter with the New York Rangers, Martin Brodeur with the New Jersey Devils, Chris Osgood of the Detroit Red Wings and Olaf Kolzig of the Washington Capitals.

Game 8: The Honor Roll

Records and Awards

Hockey awards and records have been a source of debate and trivia for as long as the game has been played. Here's your chance to have some of those "hot stove" discussions of who did what, when and where.

First Period: Who Am I?

1. I won the Conn Smythe Trophy as most valuable player in the Stanley Cup playoffs and the Calder Trophy as the best rookie the following year.

Ken Dryden won the Conn Smythe in the 1971 playoffs and was still eligible to win the Calder Trophy as rookie of the year for 1971–72.

2. I won the first four Selke awards as the best defensive forward.

Bob Gainey won the Frank Selke Trophy from 1978 to 1981.

3. I was the first winner of the Jack Adams Award who had never played in the NHL.

Scotty Bowman won the Jack Adams Award as head coach of the Montreal Canadiens in the 1976–77 season.

4. I won the highest number of consecutive Norris awards as the NHL's best defenseman.

Bobby Orr won eight straight Norris awards from 1968 to 1975.

5. I have won the Jack Adams Award as the NHL's best coach the highest number of times.

Pat Burns won the Jack Adams Award as the NHL's outstanding coach on three occasions: in 1989 with Montreal, 1993 with Toronto and 1998 with Boston.

6. We are the only players to win the Hart Trophy on two occasions without being named to the NHL First All-Star Team in the same season.

Wayne Gretzky won the Hart Trophy in 1980 and 1989 and was named as the Second All-Star Team center both times. Nels Stewart received the Hart in 1926 and 1930 prior to All-Star Team selections.

7. I am the only individual to be the first-time winner of two different NHL trophies.

Frank Nighbor was the first recipient of the Hart Trophy as the NHL's most valuable player in 1924 and in 1925 the first winner of the Lady Byng Trophy as the player to be the best example of sportsmanship and gentlemanly conduct combined with a high standard of playing ability. He also won the Lady Byng in 1926, and his outstanding Hall of Fame career included being a member of five Stanley Cup winners.

8. I am the only individual to win the Hart Trophy as the NHL's most valuable player during my last season in the NHL.

Tom Anderson of the 1941–42 Brooklyn Americans was the only player to win the Hart Trophy in his final NHL season. Ted Kennedy had been awarded the Hart Trophy for 1954–55, after which he retired, but he came back to play the last half of the 1956–57 season with the Toronto Maple Leafs.

9. I am the only person to play in the first 13 annual All-Star games, from 1947 to 1959.

Maurice "Rocket" Richard played in 13 consecutive All-Star games from 1947 to 1959. He retired before the 1960–61 season and therefore didn't take part in the All-Star Game in 1960.

10. Frank Boucher of the New York Rangers won the Lady Byng Trophy in seven of the eight years between 1928 and 1935. I was the only other player to win the Lady Byng in those eight seasons.

"Gentleman" Joe Primeau of the Toronto Maple Leafs won the Lady Byng Trophy in 1932 to interrupt Boucher's string of consecutive Lady Byng awards (and Boucher was runner-up to Primeau in 1932). Boucher was eventually given the original trophy and the NHL used a replacement.

11. I am the only player to be awarded the Art Ross Trophy as the NHL's leading scorer who has played for the Toronto Maple Leafs.

While Dickie Moore won the trophy as a member of the Montreal Canadiens on two occasions (1958 and 1959) he was the only winner to skate with the Leafs, as he played with them during the 1964–65 season. The last Maple Leaf to lead the NHL in scoring was Gordie Drillon in 1937–38, but at that point there was no award for the leading scorer in the NHL. The Art Ross Trophy was first awarded for the 1947–48 season.

12. If the Maurice "Rocket" Richard Trophy (the NHL's top goal scorer) had been presented in my playing days, I would have won the award in a record six consecutive seasons.

Phil Esposito of the Boston Bruins led the NHL in goal-scoring for six consecutive seasons from 1969–70 through to 1974–75.

13. I am the last winner of the Art Ross Trophy to wear a single-digit number on my sweater.

Bobby Orr of the Boston Bruins was awarded the Art Ross Trophy as the NHL's leading scorer for the 1974–75 season while sporting his famous number 4—and that was the last time a player wearing a single-digit number has won the NHL's scoring race.

14. I won four different individual NHL awards with the Philadelphia Flyers.

Bobby Clarke won the Bill Masterton Trophy in 1972, the Hart Trophy in 1973, 1975 and 1976, the Lester B. Pearson Award in 1973 and the Selke Trophy in 1983—all as a Flyer.

15. I am the only individual to be presented with the Jack Adams Award as the NHL's top coach in two consecutive seasons.

Jacques Demers was awarded the Jack Adams Award as the NHL's best coach for both 1986–87 and 1987–88.

16. I was the first Chicago Black Hawk to win the Hart Trophy.
Max Bentley won the Hart Trophy as a Chicago Black Hawk in 1946.

17. I am the only NHL player to receive the same individual award as a member of three NHL franchises.
Wayne Gretzky has won the Lady Byng Trophy as a member of the Edmonton Oilers (1980), the Los Angeles Kings (1991, 1992 and 1994) and the New York Rangers (1999).

18. I was the first recipient of the Jack Adams Award, having been selected as the NHL's best coach that season.
Fred Shero of the Philadelphia Flyers was the first winner of the Jack Adams Award for the 1973–74 season.

19. I am the first goaltender to be awarded both the William M. Jennings and Vezina trophies in the same NHL season.
Patrick Roy of the Montreal Canadiens won both the William M. Jennings and the Vezina for 1988–89. Beginning with the 1981–82 season, the NHL awarded the Jennings Trophy to the goaltenders on the team that allowed the fewest goals-against in the regular season, while the Vezina Trophy is presented to the individual selected as the best goaltender in the league for that season. Both Eddie Belfour of Chicago and Dominik Hasek of Buffalo have duplicated this feat.

20. I was never able to win the NHL's regular-season scoring race with the most points although I was runner-up on five separate occasions.
Maurice "Rocket" Richard

	GP	G	A	PTS
1944–45				
Elmer Lach, Montreal	50	26	54	80
Maurice Richard, Montreal	50	50	23	73
1946–47	GP	G	A	PTS
Max Bentley, Chicago	60	29	43	72
Maurice Richard, Montreal	60	45	26	71
1950–51	GP	G	A	PTS
Gordie Howe, Detroit	70	43	43	86
Maurice Richard, Montreal	65	42	24	66
1953–54	GP	G	A	PTS
Gordie Howe, Detroit	70	33	48	81

Maurice Richard, Montreal	70	37	30	67
1954–55	*GP*	*G*	*A*	*PTS*
Bernie Geoffrion, Montreal	70	38	37	75
Maurice Richard, Montreal	67*	38	36	74

*Maurice Richard missed the final three games of the 1954–55 season due to suspension.

Second Period: Multiple Choice

1. How many times has the Lady Byng Trophy been awarded to a defenseman?
a) 1   b) 2   c) 3   d) 4

   d) 4. The Lady Byng Trophy has been won by a defenseman on four occasions, all within a six-year period. Bill Quackenbush of Detroit won the award in 1949 and Red Kelly of Detroit won the award in 1951, 1953 and 1954.

2. Which of the following defensemen was the only one to win the Norris Trophy in back-to-back seasons with different NHL teams?
a) Chris Chelios   b) Paul Coffey
c) Doug Harvey   d) Bobby Orr

   c) Doug Harvey won the Norris Trophy in 1961 with the Montreal Canadiens and then again in 1962 with the New York Rangers.

3. The following four players were consecutive winners of the Calder Memorial Trophy as the NHL rookie of the year. Which of them doesn't belong with this group, based on a second unique achievement?
a) Danny Grant   b) Tony Esposito
c) Gilbert Perreault   d) Ken Dryden

   c) Gilbert Perreault. Danny Grant, Tony Esposito and Ken Dryden were all members of a Montreal Canadiens Stanley Cup-winning team the year before winning the Calder Trophy. Danny Grant was with the 1968 Montreal Cup winners and won the Calder in 1969 with Minnesota. Tony Esposito was a Canadiens Cup winner in 1969 and won the Calder in 1970 with Chicago. Dryden was a member of the Canadiens when they won the Cup in 1971 and won the Calder in 1972. Perreault played his first NHL games and won the Calder Trophy with Buffalo in 1970–71.

4. **The Boston Bruins and the Montreal Canadiens have retired the most sweater numbers (seven) of any of the NHL teams. How many of the same sweater numbers have been retired by both Boston and Montreal?**
a) 2   b) 3   c) 4   d) 5

   c) 4. Boston and Montreal have both retired sweater number 2 for Eddie Shore (Boston) and Doug Harvey (Montreal), number 4 for Bobby Orr (Boston) and Jean Beliveau (Montreal), number 7 for Phil Esposito (Boston) and Howie Morenz (Montreal) and number 9 for Johnny Bucyk (Boston) and Maurice Richard (Montreal). The other retired numbers for Boston are 3 (Lionel Hitchman), 5 (Dit Clapper) and 15 (Milt Schmidt). For Montreal, they are 1 (Jacques Plante), 10 (Guy Lafleur) and 16 (Henri Richard).

5. **Name the player who scored the most goals in one season in the 1950s.**
a) Gordie Howe   b) Bobby Hull
c) Bernie Geoffrion   d) Maurice Richard

   a) Gordie Howe scored 49 goals in 1952–53, which was the most recorded in one season in the 1950s. Gordie Howe never scored 50 goals in a season, which the other three players named here accomplished, but not during the 1950s.

6. **Which NHL arena saw the first three players record their 1,000th point in the NHL?**
a) Boston Garden   b) Chicago Stadium
c) Detroit Olympia   d) Montreal Forum

   c) Detroit Olympia. The first to record 1,000 points was Gordie Howe with an assist in a 2–0 win over Toronto on November 27, 1960. Jean Beliveau scored a goal in a 5–2 Montreal loss on March 3, 1968. On February 16, 1969, Alex Delvecchio recorded an assist in a 6–3 win over the visiting Los Angeles Kings.

7. **Which of the following Calder Trophy winners didn't score 50 goals in their rookie season?**
a) Mike Bossy   b) Joe Nieuwendyk
c) Luc Robitaille   d) Teemu Selanne

   c) Luc Robitaille scored 45 goals for the Los Angeles Kings in his rookie year, 1986–87. Selanne scored a rookie record 76 goals with the

Winnipeg Jets in 1992–93. Bossy recorded 53 goals as a rookie with the New York Islanders in 1977–78. Nieuwendyk recorded 51 goals in 1987–88 with the Calgary Flames.

8. How many times has the Calder Trophy winner been on a Stanley Cup championship team in the same season?
a) 7   b) 8   c) 9   d) 10

b) 8.

Season	Calder Trophy Winner	Stanley Cup Champions
1937–38	Cully Dahlstrom	Chicago Black Hawks
1938–39	Frank Brimsek	Boston Bruins
1939–40	Kilby MacDonald	New York Rangers
1944–45	Frank McCool	Toronto Maple Leafs
1946–47	Howie Meeker	Toronto Maple Leafs
1958–59	Ralph Backstrom	Montreal Canadiens
1962–63	Kent Douglas	Toronto Maple Leafs
1999–2000	Scott Gomez	New Jersey Devils

9. On how many occasions have the top four spots in the scoring race gone to four players on the same team?
a) 0   b) 1   c) 2   d) 3

c) 2.

Leading Scorers, 1970–71	GP	G	A	PTS
Phil Esposito, Boston	78	76	76	152
Bobby Orr, Boston	78	37	102	139
Johnny Bucyk, Boston	78	51	65	116
Ken Hodge, Boston	78	43	62	105

Leading Scorers, 1973–74	GP	G	A	PTS
Phil Esposito, Boston	78	68	77	145
Bobby Orr, Boston	74	32	90	122
Ken Hodge, Boston	76	50	55	105
Wayne Cashman, Boston	78	30	59	89

10. In the 25 years of the Original Six era (1942 to 1967) on how many occasions were no Montreal Canadiens chosen to the First or Second NHL All–Star teams?
a) 0   b) 1   c) 2   d) 3

c) 2. The only years in which no Montreal Canadiens were selected to the First or Second NHL All–Star teams of the Original Six era were its first and last seasons, 1942–43 and 1966–67.

11. During the Original Six era, how many times were all six of the NHL teams represented on either the First or Second NHL All–Star teams?
a) 0   b) 2   c) 4   d) 6

   b) 2.

NHL All–Star Teams, 1947–48

	First Team	Second Team
Goal	Turk Broda, Toronto	Frank Brimsek, Boston
Defense	Bill Quackenbush, Detroit	Ken Reardon, Montreal
Defense	Jack Stewart, Detroit	Neil Colville, New York
Center	Elmer Lach, Montreal	Buddy O'Connor, New York
Left Wing	Ted Lindsay, Detroit	Gaye Stewart, Chicago
Right Wing	Maurice Richard, Montreal	Bud Poile, Chicago

NHL All–Star Teams, 1959–60

	First Team	Second Team
Goal	Glenn Hall, Chicago	Jacques Plante, Montreal
Defense	Doug Harvey, Montreal	Allan Stanley, Toronto
Defense	Marcel Pronovost, Detroit	Pierre Pilote, Chicago
Center	Jean Beliveau, Montreal	Bronco Horvath, Boston
Left Wing	Bobby Hull, Chicago	Dean Prentice, New York
Right Wing	Gordie Howe, Detroit	Bernie Geoffrion, Montreal

12. How many times has there been a tie for the NHL scoring leader?
a) 1   b) 2   c) 3   d) 4

   c) 3.

Leading Scorers, 1961–62	GP	G	A	PTS
Bobby Hull, Chicago*	70	50	34	84
Andy Bathgate, New York	70	28	56	84
Leading Scorers, 1979–80	GP	G	A	PTS
Marcel Dionne, Los Angeles*	80	53	84	137
Wayne Gretzky, Edmonton	79	51	86	137
Leading Scorers, 1994–95	GP	G	A	PTS
Jaromir Jagr, Pittsburgh*	48	32	38	70
Eric Lindros, Philadelphia	46	29	41	70

*Awarded Art Ross Trophy with more goals

13. The Hart Trophy is awarded annually to the player judged most valuable to his team by the Professional Hockey Writers' Association. The Lester B. Pearson Award goes to the NHL's outstanding player as selected by the members of the NHL Players' Association. In the first 31 seasons that the Lester B. Pearson Award was presented (1971 through 2001), on how many occasions did different players win the Lester B. Pearson Award and the Hart Trophy?
a) 6   b) 7   c) 8   d) 9

d) 9.

Year	Hart Trophy	Lester B. Pearson Award
1971	Bobby Orr	Phil Esposito
1972	Bobby Orr	Jean Ratelle
1975	Bobby Clarke	Bobby Orr
1976	Bobby Clarke	Guy Lafleur
1979	Bryan Trottier	Marcel Dionne
1980	Wayne Gretzky	Marcel Dionne
1981	Wayne Gretzky	Mike Liut
1989	Wayne Gretzky	Steve Yzerman
2000	Chris Pronger	Jaromir Jagr

14. Who was the first Swedish-born and -trained player to win the Calder Trophy as the NHL's rookie of the year?
a) Peter Forsberg   b) Pelle Lindbergh
c) Mats Naslund   d) Borje Salming

a) Peter Forsberg of the Quebec Nordiques (Colorado Avalanche) was the NHL's rookie of the year for 1994–95. Denis Potvin of the New York Islanders was the rookie of the year when the Maple Leafs' Borje Salming played in his first NHL season of 1973–74. Steve Larmer of the Chicago Black Hawks was the Calder Trophy winner for 1982–83, which was the rookie NHL season of the Canadiens' Mats Naslund and the Flyers' Pelle Lindbergh.

15. The Hockey Hall of Fame was established in 1943 and its first inductees were honored in 1945. How many individuals were selected as the first members of the Hall of Fame in 1945?
a) 10   b) 12   c) 14   d) 16

c) 14.

The Hockey Hall of Fame's first inductees as players were Dan Bain, Hobey Baker, Russell Bowie, Charlie Gardiner, Eddie Gerard, Frank McGee, Howie Morenz, Tommy Phillips, Harvey Pulford, Hod Stuart, Art Ross and Georges Vezina. Sir Montagu (C.V.O.) Allan and Lord (G.C.B.) Stanley of Preston were the first to be honored as builders.

16. How many individuals have been selected to the First or Second All–Star teams as a member of three different NHL franchises?
a) 5   b) 6   c) 7   d) 8

b) 6.

	All–Star Selections	Regular-Season Teams
Dick Irvin	9	Chicago (1), Toronto (4), Montreal (4)
Bill Gadsby	7	Chicago (2), New York Rangers (4), Detroit (1)
Glenn Hall	11	Detroit (2), Chicago (8), St. Louis (1)
Frank Mahovlich	9	Toronto (6), Detroit (2), Montreal (1)
Paul Coffey	8	Edmonton (5), Pittsburgh (2), Detroit (1)
Wayne Gretzky	15	Edmonton (9), Los Angeles (4), New York Rangers (2)

17. How many players have had the number 9 retired in their honor by an NHL team?
a) 5   b) 6   c) 7   d) 8

b) 6. Johnny Bucyk has had his number 9 retired by the Boston Bruins, Clark Gillies by the New York Islanders, Gordie Howe by the Detroit Red Wings and Hartford Whalers, Bobby Hull by the Chicago Black Hawks and Winnipeg Jets, Lanny McDonald by the Calgary Flames and Maurice "Rocket" Richard by the Montreal Canadiens. The Toronto Maple Leafs have honored but not retired the number to recognize Charlie Conacher and Ted Kennedy.

18. Nineteen of the first 21 annual All–Star games pitted the Stanley Cup champions of the previous year against the NHL All–Stars. How many times did the All–Stars defeat the defending Stanley Cup champions?
a) 7   b) 8   c) 9   d) 10

c) 9.

NHL All–Stars vs. Stanley Cup Champions

Team	W	L	T
All–Stars	9	7	3
Montreal Canadiens	3	4	1
Toronto Maple Leafs	2	4	1
Detroit Red Wings	2	0	1
Chicago Black Hawks	0	1	0

19. Which one of the following coaches has won the Jack Adams Award?
a) **Terry Crisp**   b) **Doug MacLean**
c) **Bryan Murray**   d) **Roger Neilson**

c) Bryan Murray won the Jack Adams Award as coach of the Washington Capitals for the 1983–84 season. The other three have all placed second in voting for the award, Terry Crisp with Calgary in 1987–88, Roger Neilson with the New York Rangers in 1991–92 and Doug MacLean with the Florida Panthers in 1995–96.

20. How many defensemen have been awarded the Norris Trophy with two franchises?
a) 2   b) 3   c) 4   d) 5

b) 3. Doug Harvey, Paul Coffey and Chris Chelios have all won the Norris Trophy in two different NHL cities. Doug Harvey won it on six occasions as a member of the Montreal Canadiens between 1955 and 1961 and then a seventh time in 1962 as a New York Ranger. Paul Coffey won the award in 1985 and 1986 with the Edmonton Oilers and then again in 1995 with the Detroit Red Wings. Chris Chelios won it in 1989 with the Montreal Canadiens and in 1993 and 1996 as a Chicago Blackhawk.

Third Period: Expert Trivia

1. Name the only two players who have been selected to a First or Second NHL All–Star Team at both defense and forward.

Aubrey "Dit" Clapper of the Boston Bruins was chosen at right wing on the NHL Second All–Star Team for 1930–31 and 1934–35. Clapper was also named on defense to the First Team in 1938–39, 1939–40 and

Gordie Howe won the Art Ross and Hart Trophies on six occasions during his twenty-five seasons with the Detroit Red Wings.

1940–41 and the Second Team in 1943–44. The New York Rangers' Neil Colville was the NHL's Second Team All–Star center in both 1938–39 and 1939–40 and a defenseman in 1947–48.

2. **Name the runner-up for the Frank J. Selke Trophy in three of the first four years it was awarded and who finally won it in 1985.**

Craig Ramsay of the Buffalo Sabres was runner-up to Bob Gainey in three of the first four years the trophy was awarded and won the Selke in 1985.

3. **Name the player who won the Calder Trophy for his first season in the NHL and followed it up with the Conn Smythe Trophy in his second.**

Goaltender Roger Crozier of the Detroit Red Wings won the Calder Trophy as rookie of the year in 1965 and then won the Conn Smythe Trophy as the most valuable player in the 1966 Stanley Cup playoffs.

4. **Since the NHL began naming First and Second All–Star teams in the 1930–31 NHL season, only twice has the Hart Trophy been awarded to a player who hasn't been placed on either All–Star team. Name the players.**

Black Hawks' goalie Al Rollins won the Hart for 1953–54 and Ted Kennedy was awarded the trophy for 1954–55 as a member of the Toronto Maple Leafs. Neither was elected to an NHL All–Star team for that season.

5. **Since the 1967–68 expansion, the Art Ross Trophy has been awarded on only three occasions to a player who has scored less than 100 points in a season. When did this happen?**

In 1967–68, Stan Mikita won the scoring title with 87 points. In the lockout-shortened 1994–95 season, Jaromir Jagr won with 70 points. Jagr won again in 1999–2000 with 96 points.

6. **Which NHL team has the most retired numbers without any of the honored players being members of the Hockey Hall of Fame?**

The St. Louis Blues have retired four numbers—number 3 for Bob Gassoff, number 8 for Barclay Plager, number 11 for Brian Sutter and number 24 for Bernie Federkom—yet none of the honored players are in the Hockey Hall of Fame.

7. Name the four pairs of goalies who have both faced each other and shared the netminding in the Stanley Cup finals.

Johnny Bower (Toronto) and Terry Sawchuk (Detroit) faced each other in the 1963 and 1964 Stanley Cup finals and shared the goaltending for the 1967 Maple Leafs. Jacques Plante (Montreal) and Glenn Hall (Detroit) were opponents in 1956 and teammates during the 1969 and 1970 finals with the St. Louis Blues. Andy Moog and Grant Fuhr shared the netminding for the Edmonton Oilers in the 1984 finals and faced each other in 1988, Fuhr with the Oilers and Moog with Boston. Eddie Belfour and Dominik Hasek were the goalies for the 1992 Chicago Blackhawks and opposed each other in 1999, Hasek with Buffalo and Belfour with the Cup-winning Dallas Stars.

8. For the last 20 seasons of the Original Six era, the All–Star Game traditionally opened the season with the NHL All–Stars facing the Stanley Cup champions from the previous season. In which years did the NHL break from this tradition?

There were four breaks from the tradition. The All–Star Game was played four weeks into the season in November 1948 when Toronto played the All–Stars in a game in Chicago. In both 1951 and 1952, the First All–Star Team played the Second All–Star Team, and the 1966–67 All–Star Game was moved to the middle of the season when Montreal defeated the NHL All–Stars 3–0 in January 1967.

9. Has any individual ever won the Conn Smythe Trophy as the most valuable player to his team in the playoffs for more than one NHL franchise?

Patrick Roy won the Conn Smythe Trophy in 1986 and 1993 with the Montreal Canadiens, and in 2001 with the Colorado Avalanche.

10. Only once have three NHL defensemen who had won or would win the Norris Trophy in their careers played together on the same team. When did this happen?

The 1991–92 Los Angeles Kings had Rob Blake, Paul Coffey and Larry Robinson on defense for the conclusion of the regular season and playoffs. Robinson had won the Norris Trophy as a member of the Montreal Canadiens in 1977 and 1980. Coffey had won the Norris twice with the Edmonton Oilers (1985 and 1986) and would eventually win it again with the Detroit Red Wings in 1995. Rob Blake would go on to win it with the Los Angeles Kings in 1998.

11. Name the three Americans who have won the Norris Trophy as the NHL's outstanding defenseman.

Rod Langway was the first American to win the Norris Trophy, which he did as a member of the Washington Capitals in 1983/1984. Chris Chelios won the trophy in 1989 as a member of the Montreal Canadiens and again in 1993 and 1996 with the Chicago Blackhawks. Brian Leetch won the award in 1992 and 1997 as a New York Ranger.

12. Name the only three players to score 60 or more goals in three consecutive NHL seasons.

Mike Bossy of the New York Islanders scored 68 goals in 1980–81, 64 in 1981–82 and 60 in 1982–83. Wayne Gretzky of the Edmonton Oilers recorded 92 goals in 1981–82, 71 in 1982–83, 87 in 1983–84 and 73 in 1984–85. Brett Hull of the St. Louis Blues recorded 72 goals in 1989–90, 86 in 1990–91 and 70 in 1991–92. Five other players including Pavel Bure, Phil Esposito, Jari Kurri, Mario Lemieux and Steve Yzerman have had back-to-back seasons of 60 goals or more, but Bossy, Gretzky and Hull are the only ones to achieve this feat in three or more consecutive seasons.

13. The Toronto Maple Leafs have never had a member of their defense win the James Norris Trophy, but three Leafs have won a Norris with another NHL franchise. Can you name them?

Leonard "Red" Kelly, Pierre Pilote and Randy Carlyle.

	Norris Trophy Season(s)	*Maple Leafs Season(s)*
Red Kelly, Detroit Red Wings	1953–54	1960–61 to 1966–67
Pierre Pilote, Chicago Black Hawks	1962–63, 1963–64, 1964–65	1968–69
Randy Carlyle, Pittsburgh Penguins	1980–81	1976–77 to 1977–78

14. Name the last time that two Canadian-born players won back-to-back Calder awards as the NHL's rookie of the year.

The last time this occurred was when Luc Robitaille of the Los Angeles Kings and Joe Nieuwendyk of the Calgary Flames were back-to-back winners of the Calder Trophy as the NHL's outstanding rookie in 1987 and 1988 respectively.

15. Name the six individuals who are the all-time leaders by position selected to the First NHL All–Star Team.

Position	Player	First Team Selections
Goal	Glenn Hall	7
Defense	Ray Bourque	13
	Doug Harvey	10
Center	Wayne Gretzky	8
Left wing	Bobby Hull	10
Right wing	Gordie Howe	12

16. Name the only three players to win the Hart Trophy in their first NHL season.

Nels Stewart, Montreal Maroons, 1926; Herb Gardiner, Montreal Canadiens, 1927; and Wayne Gretzky, Edmonton Oilers, 1980.

17. Who holds the record for the highest number of goals in a single playoff year?

The record for the highest number of goals in a single playoff season is 19, which was achieved by two players. Reggie Leach of the Philadelphia Flyers was the first to score 19 goals, which he did in 16 games in the 1976 playoffs. Jari Kurri of the Edmonton Oilers also scored 19 goals in 18 games in the 1985 playoffs.

18. Name the two rookies who won the Conn Smythe Trophy in consecutive seasons.

Patrick Roy, Montreal, 1986, and Ron Hextall, Philadelphia, 1987.

19. What is the most common surname of inductees into the Hall of Fame?

There are six Smiths in the Hockey Hall of Fame, five as players and one as a builder.

	Honored Member	*Year Inducted*
Alf Smith	Right Winger, 1894–95 to 1908–09	1962
Clint Smith	Center, NHL 1936–37 to 1946–47	1991
Hooley Smith	Forward, NHL 1924–25 to 1940–41	1972
Tommy Smith	Center, 1905–06 to 1919–20	1973
Billy Smith	Goaltender, NHL 1971–72 to 1988–89	1993
Frank Smith	Organizer, Toronto Minor Hockey Programs	1962

20. Name the two winners of the Norris Trophy who have made only a single appearance on an NHL First or Second All–Star Team.

Harry Howell of the New York Rangers won the Norris Trophy and was named to the NHL's First All–Star team for 1966–67—his lone All–Star appearance in his 21-year NHL career. Randy Carlyle duplicated the feat in 1980–81 as a member of the Pittsburgh Penguins, his sole NHL All–Star appearance in a 17-year NHL career.

Overtime: Four on Four

1. Name the only four players to record their 1,000th NHL point as a member of the Maple Leafs.

Norm Ullman reached his 1,000th point on October 16, 1971, when he recorded an assist in a 5–3 loss to the New York Rangers in Toronto. Glenn Anderson recorded his 1,000th on February 22, 1993, when he scored in an 8–1 Toronto win in Vancouver. Doug Gilmour's came on December 23, 1995, when he recorded an assist in a Toronto 6–1 victory over the Oilers at Maple Leaf Gardens. Larry Murphy achieved the feat on March 27, 1996, when he scored a goal in a 6–2 win in Vancouver.

2. Name the four players to win the Lady Byng Trophy with more than one NHL franchise.

Red Kelly was awarded the Lady Byng as a member of the Detroit Red Wings in 1951, 1953 and 1954 and then as a Toronto Maple Leaf in 1961. Jean Ratelle won the Lady Byng with the New York Rangers in 1972 and then as a Boston Bruin in 1976. Marcel Dionne achieved it with the Detroit Red Wings in 1975 and then the Los Angeles Kings in 1977. Wayne Gretzky was awarded the Lady Byng Trophy on three different teams: the

Edmonton Oilers in 1980, the Los Angeles Kings in 1991, 1992 and 1994 and the New York Rangers in 1999.

3. Name the four defensemen to win the Norris Trophy while wearing number 2.

Doug Harvey, Jacques Laperriere, Brian Leetch and Al MacInnis have all won the Norris Trophy while wearing the sweater number 2.

4. Name the four players who have won the Art Ross Trophy in four or more consecutive seasons.

Player	Team	Art Ross Awards	Years
Gordie Howe	Detroit	4	1951 to 1954
Phil Esposito	Boston	4	1971 to 1974
Wayne Gretzky	Edmonton	7	1981 to 1987
Jaromir Jagr	Pittsburgh	4	1998 to 2001

Game 9: A Global Game

International Hockey

What is now considered the first World Championship took place as a demonstration tournament at the Summer Olympic Games in Belgium in April 1920. Canada tended to dominate early international matches until the 1950s, when the Soviet Union began to make noise as a hockey superpower. The past 30 years have included countless memorable moments in international hockey, including the 1972 Summit Series, the 1980 Miracle on Ice and the Czech Republic's gold medal win in the 1998 Olympics. The game also became truly inclusive in the 1998 Olympics with the addition of women's hockey as a recognized sport, and fans are eagerly anticipating both the men's and women's tournaments in the 2002 Salt Lake City Olympics.

First Period: Who Am I?

1. **I played for the 1961 world champion Trail Smoke Eaters and the Canadian national team in the 1960s. I saw my only NHL action for the St. Louis Blues in 1967–68.**
   Goaltender Seth Martin represented Canada on several occasions in the 1960s and played for the St. Louis Blues in 1967–68.

2. **I wore number 28 for Team Canada in 1972.**
   Bobby Clarke wore number 28 in the Summit Series.

3. I was the winning goaltender when the Philadelphia Flyers defeated the Soviet Red Army by a score of 4–1 on January 11, 1976.

Wayne Stephenson was in goal when the Flyers beat the Soviets on January 11, 1976.

4. We are the only two players to be members of multiple Olympic gold medal-winning and Stanley Cup-winning teams.

Viacheslav Fetisov and Igor Larionov were members of the 1984 and 1988 Soviet teams that won the Olympic gold medal and were also with the 1997 and 1998 Stanley Cup-winning Detroit Red Wings.

5. I led the scoring race with 19 points at the 1958 World Championship with the Whitby Dunlops, who captured the gold medal for Canada. I was also a member of two Stanley Cup-winning teams in spite of a very brief NHL career that included six games in the regular season and seven in the playoffs.

Connie Broden recorded 12 goals and seven assists for 19 points in seven games in the 1958 World Championship. Broden also played for the 1956–57 and 1957–58 Montreal Canadiens and is still the only individual to have been on both a gold medal team at the World Championships and a Stanley Cup winner in the same year (1958).

6. I have been a member of every gold medal-winning team in the Women's World Hockey Championships.

Geraldine Heaney is the only player who was on all seven Canadian gold medal winners in the Women's World Hockey Championships.

7. I scored the winning goal in the first game of the 1972 Summit Series.

On September 2, 1972, Valeri Kharlamov scored at 10:18 of the second period to put the Soviet Union ahead by a score of 4–2 in game one of the Summit Series. The Soviets eventually won the game 7–3.

8. I was the leading scorer for the NHL All–Stars in the three-game Challenge Cup versus the Soviet national team in February 1979.

Mike Bossy led NHL scorers with two goals and two assists for four points during the 1979 Challenge Cup, which was won by the USSR national team.

9. I scored the final goal of the game in four of Team Canada's six victories in the 1976 Canada Cup tournament.

Darryl Sittler scored Canada's 11th goal in an 11–2 victory over Finland at 15:52 of the third period on September 2 and an empty-net goal at 19:46 of the third period in Canada's 4–2 victory over Team USA on September 5. Canada's sixth goal was put in by Sittler at 19:59 of the third period in Canada's 6–0 win over Czechoslovakia in game one of the finals on September 13 and he fired the winning goal of the 1976 Canada Cup tournament at 11:33 of overtime in game two of the finals on September 15.

10. I was the leading scorer for the Soviets in the 1972 Summit Series.

Alexander Yakushev scored seven goals and added four assists for 11 points in the 1972 Summit Series.

11. I was the first European-trained player to be named to one of the annual NHL All-Star teams.

Borje Salming joined the Toronto Maple Leafs for the 1973–74 season and was elected to the NHL's Second All-Star Team the following year. Salming was named to six All-Star teams in his 17 seasons in the NHL and was elected to the Hockey Hall of Fame in 1996.

12. I was the leading scorer at the 1992 Olympic Games. (Hint: I recorded 193 points in my first 161 regular-season NHL games as a Boston Bruin.)

Joe Juneau recorded six goals and nine assists for a tournament-leading 15 points while playing eight games for Canada in the 1992 Winter Olympic Games.

13. I have never represented Canada in a Canada Cup, World Cup or Olympic tournament but was on the two gold medal-winning Canadian teams in the World Championships in 1994 and 1997.

Geoff Sanderson played for Team Canada in both the 1994 and 1997 World Championships. Rob Blake was also on both of these teams, but he did play for Canada in the 1996 World Cup and the 1998 Olympics.

14. I was in goal for Canada when they won their first World Championship in 33 years with a shootout victory over Finland in the 1994 World Championships.

Bill Ranford had an outstanding tournament as he led Team Canada to its first World Championship since the Trail Smoke Eaters gold medal performance in 1961.

15. I led Russia in scoring at the 1998 Winter Olympics.

Pavel Bure recorded nine goals in the six games he played for Russia in the 1998 Olympic Games.

16. I scored the first goal in the 1972 Summit Series between Team Canada and the USSR.

Phil Esposito scored at 30 seconds of game one on September 2, 1972, in Montreal. Canada took a 2–0 lead early in the game but ended up losing 7–3 to the Soviet Union.

17. I was the leading scorer in the 1994 Olympic Games in Lillehammer, Norway. I went on to play in the NHL with both the New York Islanders and the Los Angeles Kings.

Zigmund Palffy of Slovakia recorded three goals and seven assists for 10 points in the eight games he played during the 1994 Olympic Games and went on to become a prolific scorer in the NHL with both the New York Islanders and Los Angeles Kings.

18. I was the captain of Team Sweden in the 1976 Canada Cup. (Hint: I was the first European-trained player to be a captain in the NHL.)

Lars-Erik Sjoberg was the captain of Team Sweden in the 1976 Canada Cup and was also the captain of the Winnipeg Jets for the 1979–80 NHL season.

19. I organized the first true Canadian national hockey team for the 1963–64 season and coached the team when it represented Canada at the 1964 Winter Olympics.

David Bauer was a member of the 1944 Memorial Cup champion Oshawa Generals. He entered the priesthood and began teaching at St. Mike's in Toronto, where he coached the school team to the 1961 Memorial Cup championship. Father David Bauer went on to coach and/or manage Canada's national team from the 1964 Olympics to the demise of the program in the 1969–70 hockey season. He was inducted into the Hockey Hall of Fame as a builder in 1989.

20. I have represented the United States in all of the Women's World Hockey Championships to the end of the 2000–2001 season. (Hint: My brother won the Bill Masterton Memorial Trophy in 1997.)

Cammi Granato has represented the United States at seven Women's World Championships. She is the sister of NHL veteran Tony Granato.

Second Period: Multiple Choice

1. Which goaltender played all the games for Team Canada in 1976?
a) Ken Dryden   b) Bernie Parent
c) Gerry Cheevers d) Rogie Vachon

d) Rogie Vachon played all seven games for Team Canada in the 1976 Canada Cup.

2. Players from the WHA made up Team Canada '74, which took part in an eight-game series against the Soviets in September and early October 1974. How many games was Team Canada '74 able to win?
a) 0   b) 1   c) 2   d) 3

b) 1. Team Canada '74 won a single game over the USSR, a 4–1 win in game two, which was held in Toronto on September 19, 1974. The Soviets took the series with a record of four wins, one loss and three ties.

3. The Soviet Union's national team had four significant series against elite North American non-club teams in the 1970s (Team Canada '72, Team Canada '74, Team Canada '76 and the NHL Challenge Cup in 1979). Vladislav Tretiak participated as a member of the Soviet team in all four of these encounters. Which of the following Canadian goalies was on three of these four teams?
a) Gerry Cheevers b) Ken Dryden
c) Tony Esposito   d) Rogie Vachon

a) Gerry Cheevers played in seven of the eight games in the 1974 series and the final game of the 1979 Challenge Cup. While he didn't participate, he was also a spare goaltender on the 1976 Canada Cup team. Dryden played four games of the 1972 series and two games in the 1979 Challenge Cup, Tony Esposito played four games in the 1972 Series, and Rogie Vachon only played in the 1976 Canada Cup.

4. Which of the following members of Team Canada '76 wasn't chosen to the tournament All–Star team?
a) Bobby Clarke   b) Bobby Orr
c) Darryl Sittler   d) Rogie Vachon

a) The 1976 Canada Cup All–Star team was composed of Vachon in goal with Bobby Orr and Borje Salming of Sweden on defense. The forward line consisted of Darryl Sittler, Milan Novy of Czechoslovakia and Alexander Maltsev of the Soviet Union. Bobby Clarke wasn't chosen.

5. Who was the leading scorer for Team Canada in the 1972 Summit Series?
a) Bobby Clarke   b) Yvan Cournoyer
c) Phil Esposito   d) Paul Henderson

c) Phil Esposito.

Team Canada 1972 Scoring Leaders

	GP	G	A	PTS
Phil Esposito	8	7	6	13
Paul Henderson	8	7	3	10
Bobby Clarke	8	2	4	6
Yvan Cournoyer	8	3	2	5

6. The 1972 Canada-Russia series was held at a time when the NHL was still dominated by the Original Six teams. How many of the 35 players on Team Canada '72 came from expansion franchises?
a) 6   b) 7   c) 8   d) 9

b) 7. Only Bill Goldsworthy and J. P. Parise of the Minnesota North Stars, Bobby Clarke of the Philadelphia Flyers, Gilbert Perreault and Rick Martin of the Buffalo Sabres and Dale Tallon and Jocelyn Guevremont of the Vancouver Canucks were with expansion franchises when they were named to Team Canada '72.

7. Canada's defensive lineup for the 1976 Canada Cup may be the most impressive ever selected, but it could have been even stronger. Which of the following players wasn't on it?
a) Bobby Orr   b) Brad Park
c) Denis Potvin   d) Larry Robinson

   b) Injuries prevented Brad Park from participating in this series. The Team Canada '76 lineup included Bobby Orr, Denis Potvin, Larry Robinson, Guy Lapointe and Serge Savard. Jimmy Watson of the Philadelphia Flyers also played in two games.

8. Which country did the two leading scorers in the 1998 Olympic Games represent?
a) Canada   b) Czech Republic
c) Finland   d) Russia

   c) Teemu Selanne and Saku Koivu of Finland led the scoring race in the 1998 Winter Olympics. Selanne recorded four goals and six assists for 10 points in five games and Koivu recorded two goals and eight assists for 10 points in six games.

9. Which two of the following countries joined Canada, the Czech Republic, Finland, Russia, Sweden and the USA in the final round of the 1998 Winter Olympics?
a) Belarus   b) Germany   c) Kazakhstan   d) Slovakia

   a) Belarus and c) Kazakhstan joined the six countries named in the question for the final round of the 1998 Winter Olympics. Germany and Slovakia both missed the final round, finishing ninth and 10th.

10. Which is the only player to take part in a game against the Soviet Union in the Olympics and the 1972 Summit Series?
a) Red Berenson   b) Ken Dryden
c) Brian Glennie   d) Rod Seiling

   d) Rod Seiling played in all seven games for Canada in the 1964 Olympics and also in three games for Team Canada in the 1972 Summit Series. Ken Dryden played against the Soviets before the national team program ended in 1970, but he never played for Canada in the Olympics. Red Berenson represented Canada at the World Championships with the Belleville McFarlands in 1959 but, again, never represented Canada at the Olympics. Brian Glennie played in all seven games for Canada in the 1968 Olympics and was a member of Team Canada '72 but didn't play in the Summit Series.

11. Which two countries have the most medals in men's Olympic hockey heading into the 2002 Games?
a) Canada   b) Czechoslovakia/Czech Republic
c) USSR/Russia   d) United States

a) Canada and c) USSR/Russia

Men's Olympic Hockey Medals, 1924 to 1998

	Total Medals	Gold	Silver	Bronze
USSR/Russia	11	8	2	1
Canada	11	5	4	2
United States	8	2	5	1
Czechoslovakia/Czech Republic	8	1	4	3

12. Which of these goalies was not a member of Team Canada in the 1996 World Cup?
a) Martin Brodeur   b) Curtis Joseph
c) Bill Ranford   d) Patrick Roy

d) Patrick Roy was not a member of the Canadian team in the 1996 World Cup. Curtis Joseph and Martin Brodeur tended the net for Canada in the 1996 World Cup. Bill Ranford did not see any game action as the spare goaltender.

13. Canada pulled out of the World Hockey Championships in 1970 in a dispute over the use of professional players. When did Canada return to the championships—with a team of NHL players?
a) 1973   b) 1975   c) 1977   d) 1979

c) As part of an agreement that allowed the Canada Cup 1976 tournament to take place, Canada agreed to return to the World Championships. They played in the 1977 championship in Austria with a team made up of NHL players who had missed the playoffs. Canada finished out of the medals in fourth place.

14. Most hockey fans recall Team USA's Miracle on Ice gold medal performance during the 1980 Winter Olympics at Lake Placid. The U.S. has won the gold medal on one other occasion. Which Olympic year was it?
a) 1924   b) 1932   c) 1956   d) 1960

d) The U.S. team won the gold medal in the 1960 Games, which were held in Squaw Valley, California. In 1924 in Chamonix, France, and 1932 in

Lake Placid, New York, the U.S. placed second to Canada. In 1956 in Cortina, Italy, the U.S. placed second behind the Soviet Union.

15. When did Finland win its first medal in men's hockey at the Olympic Games?
a) 1968   b) 1976   c) 1988   d) 1998

c) Finland won the silver medal behind the Soviet Union in the 1988 Olympic Games in Calgary, their first medal ever. Finland has since won bronze in both the 1994 and 1998 Winter Olympic Games.

16. Team Canada '72 played some games besides their eight-game Summit Series with the Russians. How many additional games did they play?
a) 1   b) 2   c) 3   d) 4

c) 3. On Saturday, September 16, 1972, Canada defeated Sweden 4–1 in Stockholm, and tied them 4–4 the next day. On Saturday, September 30, Canada tied Czechoslovakia 3–3 in Prague.

17. Many Canadians have coached other national teams over the years. Who wasn't on the coaching staff of a non-Canadian team for the 1976 Canada Cup?
a) Carl Brewer b) Billy Harris c) Harry Neale d) Bob Pulford

b) Billy Harris had coached the Swedish national team and been Canada's head coach in the 1974 Summit Series between the WHA All–Stars and the Soviet national team, but he didn't take part in the 1976 Canada Cup. Carl Brewer was the co-coach of the Finnish national team for the series. Bob Pulford was the coach of the U.S. entry and he was assisted by Harry Neale.

18. Team USA had impressive bloodlines in the 1976 Canada Cup. How many of the players had fathers who had played in the NHL?
a) 3   b) 4   c) 5   d) 6

d) 6. Harvey Bennett tended goal for the Boston Bruins in 1944–45 and was the father of Harvey Jr. and Curt Bennett. Lee Fogolin's father, Lee Fogolin Sr., was in the NHL from 1948 to 1956 with the Detroit Red Wings and the Chicago Black Hawks. Gerry O'Flaherty's father, Peanuts, had played for the New York/Brooklyn Americans in the 1940–41 and 1941–42 seasons. Craig Patrick's father, Lynn, spent 10 seasons with the

New York Rangers between 1934 and 1946. Goalie Pete LoPresti's dad, Sam, had tended goal for the Chicago Black Hawks in the 1940–41 and 1941–42 NHL seasons.

19. How many individuals on Team Canada '72 had scored 50 or more goals in a single NHL season?
a) 2   b) 3   c) 4   d) 5

a) 2. Although it would quickly become a more common occurrence, at the time of the 1972 Summit Series, only six individuals had reached the 50-goal plateau in a single NHL season, and two of them played for Team Canada. Phil Esposito had reached the milestone in the two seasons preceding the series with the Boston Bruins and Vic Hadfield had reached 50 goals with the New York Rangers in 1971–72. Three other members of Team Canada '72 would later go on to score 50 goals in a single NHL season: Mickey Redmond, Rick Martin and Marcel Dionne.

20. How many individuals played for Canada in 1972 and again in 1977?
a) 2   b) 3   c) 4   d) 5

c) 4. Ron Ellis, Phil Esposito, Tony Esposito and Rod Gilbert all represented Canada in both the 1972 Summit Series and in the country's return to the World Championships in 1977.

Third Period: Expert Trivia

1. Who were the goaltenders for the final game of the 1979 Challenge Cup between the Soviet Union and the NHL All–Stars?

The Soviet Union defeated the NHL All–Stars 6–0 to win the series two games to one. The winning goalie for the Soviets was Vladimir Myshkin and the losing goalie for the NHL was Gerry Cheevers.

2. Name the four players who left Team Canada '72 in Moscow and returned to North America.

Gilbert Perreault, Rick Martin, Vic Hadfield and Jocelyn Guevremont left Team Canada and came home in 1972.

3. Name the three individuals who played on Team Canada in 1972 and 1974.

Paul Henderson created difficulties for Soviet goalie Vladislav Tretiak throughout the 1972 Summit Series.

Pat Stapleton, Paul Henderson and Frank Mahovlich played on both teams.

4. Name the three players who were named to Team Canada '72 and were not allowed to play but suited up in 1974.

Gerry Cheevers, J. C. Tremblay and Bobby Hull had been blocked from participating in the 1972 Summit Series because they'd signed contracts with WHA teams. Team Canada '74 was composed of players from WHA teams.

5. Name the six nations that took part in the first-ever Women's Olympic hockey tournament in 1998.

The USA earned the gold medal, Canada took silver and Finland captured bronze. China, Sweden and the host, Japan, rounded out the competitors.

6. Name the last time that Canada won the Olympic gold medal in men's hockey.

The Edmonton Mercurys won the Olympic gold medal in 1952.

7. What was the smallest Olympic hockey pool ever?

As a result of the Depression, the 1932 Games in Lake Placid, New York, had only four hockey teams: Canada, the U.S., Poland and Germany.

8. Which two club teams represented the Soviet Union in the 1975–76 NHL-Soviet Super Series? Which NHL club teams did they play and what were the results?

The two clubs from the USSR were the Central Red Army and the Soviet Wings.

1975–76 NHL Soviet Super Series

Sunday, December 28, 1975	Central Red Army 7 at New York Rangers 3
Monday, December 29, 1975	Soviet Wings 7 at Pittsburgh Penguins 4
Wednesday, December 31, 1975	Central Red Army 3 at Montreal Canadiens 3
Sunday, January 4, 1976	Soviet Wings 6 at Buffalo Sabres 12
Wednesday, January 7, 1976	Soviet Wings 4 at Chicago Black Hawks 2
Thursday, January 8, 1976	Central Red Army 5 at Boston Bruins 2
Saturday, January 10, 1976	Soviet Wings 2 at New York Islanders 1
Sunday, January 11, 1976	Central Red Army 1 at Philadelphia Flyers 4

9. Name the three players on the Team USA entry in the 1976 Canada Cup who went on to become NHL general managers.

Mike Milbury, Lou Nanne and Craig Patrick played in the 1976 Canada Cup and went on to become GMs in the NHL.

10. There were five Canada Cup tournaments between 1976 and 1991. Each involved teams representing six countries, but on one occasion the lineup of participating countries was different from what it was in the other four. When was it and what was that change?

Canada, the USSR, Czechoslovakia, Sweden and the United States took part in all five Canada Cups in 1976, 1981, 1984, 1987 and 1991. Finland took part in four of the tournaments, but West Germany replaced it in 1984. West Germany had finished higher than Finland in the 1983 World Championships to qualify but experienced little success in its only appearance in the Canada Cup, achieving a single tie with Czechoslovakia during five round-robin games.

11. Name two similarities in Team Canada's first victories over the Soviet national team in 1972 and 1974.

Both teams first won games in game two of their series, played at Maple Leaf Gardens in Toronto, by a score of 4–1.

12. Name the seven players on Team Canada '72 who didn't see any playing time in the eight-game series against the Russians.

Goaltender Ed Johnston, defensemen Bobby Orr (who was injured), Jocelyn Guevremont and Brian Glennie, and forwards Dale Tallon, Rick Martin and Marcel Dionne didn't play in the Summit Series.

13. Who were the oldest members of Team Canada '72, '74 and '76?

Goalie Ed Johnston was the oldest member of Team Canada '72. He was two months short of his 37th birthday during the 1972 Summit Series. At 46, Gordie Howe was the oldest member of Team Canada '74 and 37-year-old Bobby Hull was the oldest member of Team Canada '76.

14. In the five Canada Cup tournaments, only once did a country manage to go through the entire series (round robin and playoffs) undefeated. Which country achieved this feat and in which tournament did it occur?

Team Canada went undefeated in the 1991 Canada Cup tournament with a record of six wins and two ties in the eight games played, 3–0–2 during the round robin and three straight victories in the playoffs.

15. Name the seven players with NHL experience who joined Canada for the 1988 Winter Olympics in Calgary.

Andy Moog and Randy Gregg of the Edmonton Oilers, Brian Bradley and Jim Peplinski of the Calgary Flames, Ken Yaremchuk of the Toronto Maple Leafs, Tim Watters of the Winnipeg Jets and Steve Tambellini of the Vancouver Canucks all played for Canada at the 1988 Olympics.

16. Name the only two defensemen to play for Canada in all three of the following tournaments: the 1991 Canada Cup, the 1996 World Cup and the 1998 Olympic Games.

Eric Desjardins and Scott Stevens played in all three.

17. When was the first time that Canada did *not* win the gold medal in hockey at the Winter Olympic Games?

Great Britain won the gold medal in 1936.

18. Who did the United States defeat in the final game of the 1980 Olympics to capture the gold medal?

The USA defeated Finland 4–2 in the final game to win the 1980 gold medal. Many recall Team USA's 4–3 upset over the Soviet Union that allowed the Americans to capture the gold, but they also had to defeat Finland in the last game of the tournament to take home the medal.

19. Name the three members of the 1998 Canadian women's Olympic hockey team who have brothers who have played in the NHL.

Jennifer Botterill's brother Jason has played for the Dallas Stars, Atlanta Thrashers and Calgary Flames. Judy Diduck's brother Gerald has been a member of the New York Islanders, Montreal Canadiens, Vancouver Canucks, Chicago Blackhawks, Hartford Whalers, Phoenix Coyotes, Toronto Maple Leafs and Dallas Stars. Manon Rheaume's brother Pascal has played for New Jersey and St. Louis.

20. **Name the five other members of Team Canada '72 who were on the ice when Paul Henderson scored with 34 seconds remaining in game eight of the Summit Series.**

Yvan Cournoyer, Phil Esposito, Serge Savard, Pat Stapleton and Ken Dryden were on the ice when Paul Henderson scored The Goal.

Overtime: Four on Four

1. **Name the countries that Canada defeated to win its four Canada Cup titles.**

In 1976, Canada downed Czechoslovakia two games to none. In 1984, Canada triumphed over Sweden two games to none. In 1987, Canada defeated the Soviet Union two games to one. In 1991, Canada was victorious over the United States two games to none. The only time Canada didn't win the Canada Cup was in 1981, when they lost the one-game final 8–1 to the Soviet Union.

2. **Who was the captain of Team Canada '72?**

Phil Esposito took on the role as the series went on, but there was no officially appointed captain on Team Canada in 1972. The four assistant captains were Phil Esposito, Frank Mahovlich, Stan Mikita and Jean Ratelle.

3. **Name the four NHL players that Harry Sinden and John Ferguson invited to Team Canada '72 who declined for various reasons.**

Goaltender Ed Giacomin of the New York Rangers was unable to play due to knee problems. Dallas Smith of the Boston Bruins had to remain with his off-season farm. Walt Tkaczuk had hockey school commitments. Jacques Laperriere didn't join the team because his wife was pregnant.

4. **Name the only four countries that have won medals in the Women's World Hockey Championships to date.**

Canada has won gold seven times, the U.S. has won seven silvers, Finland has won six bronze medals and Russia has won the bronze once.